A WOMAN'S GUIDE

TO SURVIVING IN A MAN'S WORLD

How *One Woman*
Survived and Thrived
Despite the
Good Old Boys

ANNE COVEY

ARCHWAY
PUBLISHING

Archway Publishing books may be ordered through booksellers or by contacting:

Archway Publishing
1663 Liberty Drive
Bloomington, IN 47403
www.archwaypublishing.com
1 (888) 242-5904

ISBN: 978-1-4808-9258-3 (sc)
ISBN: 978-1-4808-9259-0 (e)

Library of Congress Control Number: 2020912544

Print information available on the last page.

Archway Publishing rev. date: 07/16/2020

I dedicate this book to my loving husband, best friend, and soul mate. He has been my inspiration and number-one cheerleader. Without his support and encouragement, I could not have written this book.

INTRODUCTION

Since the day that God created Eve from Adam's rib, men have ruled the world. It has always been a man's world and always will be. Men enjoy the power they have over women and are not about to give that power away anytime soon.

Being born a male automatically gives you the power of belonging to the preferred gender. Nothing has changed, and nothing ever will.

When I was a toddler at age three or four, my grandparents would come over to our house to pick up my brother for the day and sometimes the whole weekend. My brother was two years older.

I was never able to understand why they chose to take my brother every time and never me. I was never allowed to go. Every time they came to pick my brother up, I would get my hopes up that this would be the day I would also get to go with them. Every weekend, I was turned down and told no. When it was time for them to leave, I would stand at the door and cry and plead for them to take me. My pleas fell on deaf ears. My sobs went unnoticed as they loaded my brother into the front seat of the car, where he sat between them.

As they left the driveway, my grandfather would give me a sharp toot of the horn, while all three would wave goodbye. As I stood there by that door, I would wonder why I could never go with them. Why did my brother get to go with them every time? After thinking for a while, I realized that my brother could go because he was a boy, and I was not. He was not only a boy but also their first grandchild. He would forever reign supreme while I would always be looking out the window, waiting for my turn, which would never happen.

Being left behind because I was not a boy is just one example of how boys learn from an early age that being a male makes them better than females. It plays out in families across the nation. Giving boys preference over girls was especially true in the sixties when I was growing up, and in many families, it still is.

I clearly remember a phone call that my father received from his nephew. His nephew was calling him to let him know that his first child had just been born, and it was a girl. My father congratulated him, and that made him happy. He went on to tell my father when he called his dad to let him know that he was a grandfather for the first time, the first words that came out of his mouth were to ask if it was a boy. When his father heard that it was a little girl, there was silence on the other end. After a long, awkward silence, his father told him to call him back when he had a boy—such a cold, callous remark. So many years later, I still remember my father telling me that story. Many men were outwardly disappointed when their firstborn was not a boy.

In some cases, a family would keep having babies until they had a boy, often blaming the wife for not having a son.

Growing up we lived near a farmer who was a Good Old Boy. He had three daughters and one son much younger than his sisters. The youngest daughter was a friend of mine. She often remarked that she was a disappointment to her father This always surprised me when she said this. I thought she was a daughter any man would be proud of. She was a cheerleader in high school and served as Secretary for our Senior class. She was smart and very likable. One day I asked her why she was a disappointment to her father. She told me he wanted a boy and instead got another daughter; she was his third daughter and he no longer could contain his disappointment. Several years after her birth, he was at last blessed with a son. However, being told that she was a disappointment to her father has haunted her and will for the rest of her life.

There are many different examples of how parents treat their sons like they matter more to them than their daughters. It bolsters their male egos when they hear their parents say such things as, "She is only a girl," or "Never let a girl beat you," and let us not forget my favorite, "Boys will be boys."

Growing up, I was always told not to upset my brother. He ruled at our house, continually getting his way and receiving privileges that I never received. This behavior stoked his ego even more. Little did they know they were creating a future member of the Good Old Boys' Club, and he was well on his way. I never held it against my brother; it was not his fault how my parents treated him. It was acceptable behavior for the time, and my parents did the best they could. My father treated me as daddy's little girl when my brother was not around. I know that my dad loved me, unlike my friend.

CHAPTER 1

What Exactly Is the Good Old Boys' Club?

According to *Merriam-Webster*, it is a simple system in which wealthy men with the same social and educational background help one another. It is sometimes known as the Old Boy Network. Whatever you choose to call it, nothing good has ever come from this club.

While the definition certainly is correct, I must add that you do not need to be wealthy to join this club. The membership of the Good Old Boys' Club is staggering, and it is still growing every day. This all-encompassing club has members from every walk of life, age, color, and background. We sometimes think of the Good Old Boys' Club membership as a venue for upper-class, white-collar men. While most of the club members fit that ideal, it is not exclusively theirs.

Often, you will see a member of the Good Old Boys' Club

working in a restaurant. The most likely person to abuse or bully a woman is perhaps a male manager or assistant manager. It is not uncommon for these bullies to abuse their power over the women by offering them better schedules in exchange for sexual favors. If the Good Old Boy does not get the liberties he has asked for, then there is sure to be a punishment for the waitress. The waitress may see her hours reduced, or she might have to work an undesirable shift, leading her to quit rather than give in to the manager's demands. Repeating this pattern of behavior, the Good Old Boy will quickly dwindle his staff of waitresses to only those who will give him sexual favors. This practice of blackmail occurs day after day all over the United States—and most likely across the globe. Every time you have a Good Old Boy wielding power over a woman, you can count on some form of abuse. I believe that the Good Old Boys cannot help themselves, even if they try. Of course, we know that they will not make any attempt to change. From the bottom of the food chain right up to the top, the behavior is very much the same.

Do not be surprised if you run into Good Old Boys in religious organizations as well. Nothing is sacred to a Good Old Boy; he will use the New Testament verse from the Bible that says wives should be submissive to their husbands. He will run with that Bible verse in hand and use it to his advantage. Good Old Boys have no shame. Their desire to control women is inherent. If the boys can't eliminate the women from their work environment, they have no other choice but to manage them.

The Good Old Boys' Club will touch everyone at one time or another. In high school, for example, the boys on the football team were often allowed to attend an urgent practice during school hours and miss classes. The cheerleaders were never permitted to miss classes; only the boys on the football team enjoyed that privilege.

One thing the Good Old Boys are famous for is protecting one another by covering for others. They always have one another's back, no matter what the situation is.

Women have a long way to go to achieve equality with men. Men dominate in the executive world; the boardroom is almost always full of men. The positions of power in the Fortune 500 companies consist of Good Old Boys who are hired by Good Old Boys. That is not to say that women are totally absent, there are very few.

Women can bump their heads on the glass ceiling for only so long before it begins to crack. There is a saying that has been around for many years: "It's not what you know; it's who you know." No one has ever made it to the top on their own. You need someone to promote you and teach you how men do business. You must act like the men to compete with the men. It is a dirty business, so you should know what you're getting yourself into before you begin the journey.

In the '50s and '60s, men-only clubs were in favor; the membership was also all white males. In this respect, we have come a long way, at least on the surface. The Old Boy Network is a way for men to provide favors, give information, and help one another by using their influence to get things done.

Most business deals are closed on the golf course or at a bar—where the Good Old Boys are free from prying eyes, and no one is around to hear them. The Good Old Boys keep within their peer group to make sure they all stick together and form tight bonds.

When I was working for a large firm as a financial planner,

the men went on golf outings once a week, usually on Friday. This outing was a men-only event. When the manager of my district invited my top client to go golfing with him, I assumed that I would also attend. Because this was my client, I thought I should be there. The manager had other ideas and chose to exclude me. On other occasions, this manager golfed with top clients of the men in the office, and they, too, were invited to participate. Of course, this is unfair and should not be allowed to happen. You must pick your battles because there are many, and I chose not to make this one of them.

When you experience a situation that is unfair and sexually biased, you need to speak up. Be confident, have your facts clearly defined, and without emotion, state the points that concern you and why they do. Crying and complaining is never the answer. If all you do is complain and you do not report the problem, you are setting yourself up for more of the same. No one likes a negative person, and that is how you will be perceived.

When dealing with Good Old Boys, learn how they do business, always be positive, and show them that you are a strong woman. Set up boundaries and let them know what behaviors you will not tolerate. And never, under any circumstances, ever, show fear or let them see you cry.

Good Old Boys will respect a strong woman who acts professionally, is confident of her abilities, and pulls her weight getting the job done.

It can be tragic if a woman marries a Good Old Boy, thinking he will change. A Good Old Boy will never change; he only becomes worse. While you are dating a Good Old Boy, he is putting his best foot forward. If he exhibits dangerous behavior, don't miss that red flag. It is easy to make excuses for the way a

Good Old Boy acts, but the only one you're fooling is yourself. Don't live in denial. If he is abusive and demanding before you get married, no marriage certificate will convince him to act like a gentleman. Not all Good Old Boys are abusers, but many are. Once a jackass, always a jackass, and you deserve better than that.

If you discover that you have married an abusive Good Old Boy, the sooner you leave, the better. The longer you stay, the harder it becomes to break free. It is not easy to leave an abuser; they will make it very difficult for you to do so. They have exceptionally delicate egos, and they do not like to lose to a woman. That is most likely where the comment "keep her barefoot and pregnant" came from. There is no doubt a member of the Good Old Boys' Club coined that phrase.

To survive in a man's world, you must never let your guard down. You may be thinking you are working with more sophisticated men because your college degree allowed you to gain employment in a professional workplace, but that is no guarantee that you will not encounter Good Old Boys while at work. The fact is that you are more likely to work with Good Old Boys in that environment. Men who fill these high-profile positions have massive egos and can be more manipulative. Remember that most of the club members are wealthy men, generally in white-collar jobs. That is not to say that all white-collar men are Good Old Boys or that men who work in manual labor professions are not Good Old Boys; it just means you should keep your guard up. If you find yourself working for a Good Old Boy, run—don't walk. The situation can spiral out of control very quickly.

Young boys learn from the behavior of their fathers. To

come across a Good Old Boy in grade school is not unusual. An excellent example of that is an incident that occurred with my daughter in middle school. A classmate lured her into an empty classroom, cornered her, put his hands under her sweater, began to feel her breasts, and tried to pull her jeans down when she started to scream. A teacher came running, and he saw the two of them alone in the room. Of course, the boy denied doing anything wrong when the principal intervened. His father was called and asked to come for a meeting with the principal.

When his father walked into the room, it soon became apparent why this boy acted the way he did. His father was dressed in an expensive suit and had an air of superiority about him. He made it clear that his time was valuable, as he was a lawyer. He went on to say that he didn't have time for childish pranks and asked why he was there. The principal began to tell him what his son had done, and the arrogant father interrupted him and asked, "Did you see this happen?" The response was no that he had not seen it happen but that the teacher, who was present in the office, had run to the empty classroom when he heard the screams. The father then turned to the teacher and asked, "Did you see it happen?" without allowing the teacher to finish telling him when he came into the room, his son was standing by the victim who was crying uncontrollably. The father became even more arrogant if that is possible. He said, "So you didn't see it either?" Making a grand gesture of leaving, the overbearing Good Old Boy lawyer/father finished it off with, "If you didn't see it, then it didn't happen, and that will hold up in a court of law," slamming the door when he left to show the case was closed.

The news is full of stories about sexual misconduct from politicians, athletes, movie stars, CEOs, priests, and many more.

Hearing these stories makes you think that this behavior has become an epidemic. However, that is not the case; the fact is the Good Old Boys have been around since the beginning of time and have sexually exploited women all along. The reason we think this is a new behavior is that we hear about it more than we ever have. No longer is it kept a secret.

Is it any wonder men grow up to be chauvinistic and try to keep women suppressed? They desperately want to control women and prevent them from any form of job advancement, particularly in those jobs that offer power and decision making. Throughout history, men learned that women have their roles, which were, for the most part, submissive ones. That is why the Good Old Boys have the impression if a woman is to attend one of their meetings, it should only be to serve coffee.

Some things never change, and that is why this is still going on today. It does not appear that it will stop anytime soon. Good Old Boys have a death grip on the control of women.

The most significant and most noticeable difference between the genders is the work environment. Most men still do not want women in their world, especially their work environment. The inequality of the sexes is still very noticeable, very few women hold positions that wield power and pay the big bucks. There are exceptions, of course, but for the most part, not very many.

You may ask why this inequality still exists. There is a straightforward explanation for that. Those sitting at the table, making the decisions for hiring and promotions, are all male. When deciding to fill an opening or give a promotion, these men prefer to give those jobs to people who are most like themselves. They are more likely to hire a man with less experience and fewer skills than a woman who is highly skilled and has many years of experience. They will keep that Good Old Boy Network alive and well.

If a woman should slip into their work environment, and she is the only woman at their meeting, the men will undoubtedly expect her to make and serve them coffee. The fact that she has the same job description as all the other men will go unnoticed. The fact she is a woman will be cause enough for the Good Old Boys to expect her to be submissive and serve them.

Early in my career, I found myself to be the only woman at a meeting with my peers. It came as no surprise to me when I was asked to serve the coffee. However, my response was very unexpected. I told them that I did not know how to make coffee. At my house, my husband made the coffee.

Not all men are chauvinistic. Not all belong to the Good Old Boys' Club. Some are gentlemen who respect women and treat them on equal terms. Although you may have to look hard for them, they are out there. My husband and son are perfect examples.

I worked with some men who were gentlemen, and I enjoyed working with them. Please do not get the impression that I am lumping all men into one category because that is not the case. Unfortunately, so many men fit into the Good Old Boys' Club, they dominate the population.

The Good Old Boys' Club has built a solid and impenetrable glass ceiling, hoping to prevent women from succeeding in the business. Do not let that stop you from trying. You may have to hit your head on the glass ceiling a few times, but you will be able to crack it if you are determined to do so.

CHAPTER 2

What Exactly Is the Glass Ceiling?

What is the glass ceiling, and why is it called that? A glass ceiling is a metaphor used to represent an invisible barrier. The glass ceiling will allow you to look through it and see the high-powered jobs, jobs that do exist. However, the glass barrier also prevents you from reaching those opportunities. The phrase became popular in the '80s and is still a topic of discussion today.

Often, you will hear people say it is invisible and therefore does not exist. Women who say this are women who have confidence and drive and will also not take no for an answer. If anyone is cracking that glass ceiling, it is sure to be a woman like that.

Those women who believe it is real and not just a metaphor are also the women who will be stifled by the glass ceiling. Just as with everything in life, everyone will see it differently and will react in her own way. Both believe their theory to be correct. Perception is reality; what is real to one is not to another.

One would think that women's equality would have progressed much further than it has by now. You might even ask why we still talk about this. Thanks to the efforts of the Good Old Boys' Club, I believe that we have gone backward on that front. Men will always keep women suppressed and keeping them under the glass ceiling is a learned behavior and well accepted in the corporate culture. Things happen with a nod and a wink, and the Boys' Club will do what they want and get away with it. Especially if women tolerate the abuse when it is endured, without complaint, why would they stop? The Good Old Boys' business practices are detrimental to women and affect women of all colors, ages, and socioeconomic standings. No one is exempt from this phenomenon; it is an equal opportunity problem.

The Good Old Boys vastly outnumber the gentlemen, especially in the work environment. There is very little chance that they will go away. Their foothold is so strong the only defense women possess is a potent offense. The only way to develop that is through diligence and knowing all you can about the Good Old Boy, what makes him tick, and what his hot buttons are.

Because you can't see the glass ceiling does not mean it is not there. It is the glass ceiling that reserves the influential, high-paying jobs for the men while keeping the gender disparity thriving. Privilege is what allows this to happen; men are born with those rights because they are born male. Men hold the glass ceiling intact partly by discriminatory hiring and promotions.

We no longer see blatant discrimination because of strict

corporate policies. Many of those are on paper only; men can quickly get around them with subtle bias.

Studies show that a higher percentage of women graduate from college than men. So, why is it that men remain in control? Could it be that women themselves are to blame? In some ways, without knowing it, many women are responsible for their failure to rise to the top. One reason is women don't own their power to lead. They are insecure and not assertive enough. This premise could be brought on by the Good Old Boys in the first place. Women have seen them and felt them controlling their work environment and do not want to rock the boat. They are afraid of the consequences and the possibility of physical abuse; although that rarely happens in the work environment, for some women, it is a real fear.

Women have also been known to be more risk-averse about their experiences or upbringing than men and will shy away from conflict. Choosing to make their male boss happy and to please them is more comfortable and safer than speaking up.

Women have learned survival traits, such as submissiveness, passivity, and dependence. Whether they are real or preconceived, women must fight to reject these traits; they are not conducive to leadership and show a weakness that prevents respect. Some might even say that women will need to disassociate from their gender and act as men do. They believe the theory of "If you can't beat them, join them," is the answer. While this is true in part, I believe that women can accomplish anything they set their minds to and still preserve their feminine side. Learning how men work can be advantageous, but you need not become one of the boys.

Men have many advantages, privileges, and rights that

women do not have, and the Good Old Boys know how to take advantage of all of them. One of them is the burden of child-care. Not only do women have babies, but it usually falls on the woman to be the one to miss work to take the children to the doctor, stay home with them when they are sick, or attend school events. All of this makes women less flexible, and that gives the men another unfair advantage.

There are laws in place to protect women's rights; the only problem is getting the Good Old Boys to follow these laws. If a woman files a complaint regarding a Good Old Boy mistreating her, she is often not heard but instead ignored. Most likely, she will have to report the incident to another Good Old Boy. This process is problematic, often making the situation worse, rather than better. The woman is sure to experience retribution in one form or another, and her work environment will soon become hostile. She may even lose her job because of a made-up excuse, such as poor performance, a bad attitude, or downsizing. None of this is true, but the Good Old Boys will get away with it because they answer to Good Old Boys who will cover their backs at all cost.

The fear of retribution is the reason why most women will not report any abuse they experience. Women feel they have no voice and are powerless in making changes. Women feel compelled to put up with atrocious behavior, and the Good Old Boys remain in control. Men will continue to receive preferential treatment, and they will always have the backs of their cohorts.

It is the Good Old Boys who have constructed the glass ceiling, and it is the Good Old Boys who keep it impenetrable. They have as many ways of preserving the glass ceiling as there are stars in the sky.

In my twenty-five years in the business world, I have experienced many of the ways they preserve the glass ceiling. I hope to reach out to women of every age and tell them my story, letting them know what to expect and how to deflect the assaults. If I can keep just one woman from falling prey to the antics of the Good Old Boys, I will have done my job.

The following stories are about men who belong to the Good Old Boys' Club and have negatively impacted my career and my life.

CHAPTER 3

The Family Glass Ceiling

Growing up in a house with both an older brother and a younger brother had its ups and downs. Being in the middle did not help. While the boys had privilege just for being males, I did have one advantage over them: I was a daddy's girl. There was no denying that. I knew my father loved me and wanted to protect me; he also had preconceived ideas regarding my future. He had a way of letting me know what he expected and did it lovingly. He was a true believer in the traditional roles of males and females. It was hard for him to accept the fact that I played on a girls' softball league, and he rarely attended any games. I was the pitcher on my team and had a wicked windmill pitch. I could also hit the ball far enough to have many home runs, and he never seemed proud of me for this. That was strange because I knew he loved me. It took me a while, but I finally figured it out when my picture was in the local paper for pitching a "no-hitter." I was excited and put in on the refrigerator like children would do with their A+ homework assignments. My father took it down and told me to hang it in my bedroom because he didn't want it to upset my older brother if he saw it. When I asked him why, he told me it was because my brother did not do well in sports, and I was a girl, so he would feel bad if he saw it. I am sure this was because of his strong old-fashioned feelings about gender roles.

Nevertheless, it upset me, and I ripped up my picture and threw it away. Having my photo in the paper no longer was exciting. I was crushed but determined to continue playing softball and be the best girl softball player I could be.

My parents were not doing my brother any favors by shielding him from everything that might hurt his ego. As he grew up to be an adult, he continued to expect that protection—maybe because it was all he knew. When you treat your child differently than the other children, the child begins to think that way of life is normal.

In many ways, I could see my brother becoming addicted to having his way; he enjoyed being treated better than me—and for that matter, everyone else. He didn't know any better. He was unaware that his sister was also important because our parents raised him to believe that he was the best at everything and the most important and should always come first.

I never resented him for this attitude while growing up. It was not his fault; our parents are to blame because they taught him his behaviors and fed his ego.

In a way, there was a glass ceiling in my home while growing up; I could see all the privileges my brother received, but there was this invisible barrier in place, preventing me from receiving them as well. I just could not break through that family glass ceiling that was present all my life.

My father was very rigid when it came to gender expectations. I continued to play softball and was envious of my teammates when their parents came to all the games. I never held it against my father, because I knew he was not trying to be nasty; he just felt strongly about his beliefs. My grandparents—yes, the ones who took my brother for all those outings—also felt the same way. They never attended any of my games but were at every one of my male cousin's games. I guess this feeling was for all extracurricular activities. Both my older brother and I played in the high school band. There were concerts, parades, and football games that we performed at. And all were attended by both my parents and grandparents. That was until my brother graduated, and they decided there was no longer any reason to go. I overheard my grandfather saying that he would miss going to these events now that my brother had graduated. In the last two years of high school, I had no one attending to watch me perform, and that was fine with me; after all, I was just a girl.

I experienced the same gender-biased attitude when it came to college. The message was that girls do not go to college; they get married and have families. I was looking at a possible scholarship based on my SAT score and my grades. But what was the use of applying when I could not go? Because I was a good girl and always tried to do the right thing, I did not pursue the scholarship. I graduated in June and got married the following January. I am still happily married forty-six years later. I also got my degree in finance, and even though I had to wait, it was worth it.

Not having a college degree can make your career choices

very dismal. I spent too many years waiting tables and doing other low-paying jobs. I wanted more than that. When both of my children were in junior high and became self-sufficient, it was my turn. I was determined to get more out of life by getting a better job. I loved waiting tables, and honestly, I would miss it. The appeal of becoming a professional in one of the fields I loved had me determined to achieve my goal. I just had to decide which area to pursue.

Psychology was top on my list. When I found out how many full-time years of schooling it would require, and having two teenagers and bills to pay, I knew it would be daunting. Psychology was not an option; I had to eliminate it and go on. The next choice was a financial adviser. I loved working with math, and I would be able to help people, which would satisfy my interest in psychology. After careful research, I settled on pursuing a job as a financial adviser. There was just one minor detail that would be in the way of my plans. Firms required their financial planners to have a bachelor's degree to be hired. That could be a problem since I did not hold that degree, but with determination and creativity, I was sure it would not be impossible.

CHAPTER 4

Alistair

That brings us to my first story, the story of when I met Alistair, the manager of a financial planning company. I called his firm to set up an appointment for an interview, thankful they did not screen their candidates over the phone. I made an appointment for the following Friday, which gave me just three days to plan my strategy. I was expecting a pompous Good Old Boy, and a Good Old Boy was what I got. He fit the definition so well they could use his picture in the dictionary as a perfect example. Alistair was in his late forties and trying desperately to look thirty; however, he failed miserably at the attempt. My first impression of Alistair was that he seemed very dictatorial. It was Alistair's way or the highway. Alistair thought he was right, even when he was wrong. When I first met Alistair, I could see that he was confident to the point of being narcissistic, and I am sure *Pompous* was his middle name. He had a most unsavory appearance that made me want to go home and shower after just sitting across his desk from him.

After talking with him for a few short minutes, I was sizing him up to learn what his weakness was and what was important to him. I also learned what pushed his buttons and what he wanted most from his job. I guess that psychology class was worthwhile and paying off. I learned that Alistair always had to be right, that anything said or done that was good was his idea and winning was necessary at all costs. I knew how to use this information to my advantage. After a few more minutes of pleasantries, Alistair decided it was time to begin my interview. He established that I was there to apply for the financial adviser position and continued to read my résumé. Just as I had anticipated, Alistair immediately focused on my level of education. He read more of my résumé and stopped, thinking about it longer than I thought was necessary before he dramatically threw the résumé down on his desk. Pausing for effect, he took off his glasses, leaned forward, and with a smirk on his face, asked me, "Am I reading this right? Is high school graduate your highest level of education?"

As he sat back in his chair, crossing his arms and looking very important, I replied that he was correct and challenged him with a question he did not see coming. "Does it matter?" I asked ever so innocently. "It couldn't possibly be that important, could it?"

Alistair's reaction was just what I had hoped it would be. With his face turning bright red and beads of sweat popping out on his bald little head, he spat out the words one at a time, trying to control his outrage, "Of course, it is important."

As Alistair attempted to compose himself, I told him, "In my opinion, selling my services as a financial adviser is no different than any of the other things I have sold." I had been the top sales representative in every company I had ever worked for, and I had a pile of awards to prove it.

Alistair had to take time to think this over; he had never dealt with this kind of challenge before. After much thought, he proudly told me, "I doubt you would be capable of passing the Series 7 licensing exam. All my financial planners hold at least a bachelor's degree, many a master's or even a doctorate. How can you possibly expect to pass such an arduous exam without a college degree? The thought of you passing this exam is laughable."

I allowed him to revel in his superiority for a few minutes, watching to see just how pretentious he could become. At the right moment, I jumped right in with a bit of attitude myself. I looked Alistair right in the eye, showing no fear, and I asked him, "If I pass the exam, would you hire me?" This question seemed to shock Alistair. He never saw it coming, because it was a bold question after he had already told me that he thought I was not capable of passing the exam. I told him, "I am confident that I can ace the exam."

He need not have laughed so hard. It was unbecoming to him as a manager. I ignored his laughter and proceeded to ask him once more, "Would you hire me if I pass the exam?"

Alistair was so sure that I was not capable or smart enough to pass the exam that he eagerly agreed.

Alistair said, "Yes, I would hire you if you secured your Series 7 license and the other licenses necessary to work as a financial adviser." He then started to laugh diabolically, which sent shivers down my spine.

It was unheard of for anyone to be a financial adviser with only a high school diploma, and I was aware of that. My objective

was to make him feel in control as if I would let that happen.
I also had to let him think it was his idea to hire me if I passed
the exam.

Before applying for the position of a financial adviser, I had
a strong background in sales and sales management, and as far
as I was concerned, that would be enough. I would learn the rest
while on the job.

Alistair puffed out his chest as if to remind me that he was
the alpha male in the company. Full of arrogance, he again
told me that I would never be able to pass the exam, which was
necessary to trade stocks and bonds—a large part of financial
planning. It was the highest level of license for the position that
I had applied for.

A Series 6 license was what most of his advisers held. It was
a much easier exam to pass and would still allow you to do most
of the financial operations.

I reassured him that if I tried and failed, I would go away
and never bother him again.

By then, Alistair was very motivated, he was the man, and
he was in control. Alistair excused himself from the room, saying that he was going to get me the materials I would need to
study for the exam, and while he was at it, he would sign me
up for the class that I was to take since it would prepare me for
the exam. I was not sure what to expect, and I waited for him
to return. When Alistair came back, he was carrying a large
pile of books; one of them seemed to be four inches thick and
the most important of them all. Alistair set the collection on
his desk. He picked up the most prominent book and handed
it to me. Alistair told me this was my study guide, while the
smaller one was a book of practice tests that I could take while

studying. After pushing the other books aside, Alistair handed me a printout; it contained an address and a schedule. He told me that it was the information I would need to attend the study class. Feeling a bit overwhelmed, without looking at it, I folded it up and placed it inside the thicker book.

Noticing the additional books sitting on his desk, I asked him if they were for me as well. With a devious smile, he replied that they were indeed for me. However, he would hang on to them. If I didn't pass the Series 7 exam, there would be no need for me to have them. I replied, "Will I receive them when I bring you the certificate for passing the Series 7 exam?" and he confirmed that when I brought him the results showing I had passed the Series 7 exam, he would give them to me at that time. The devious smile faded from his face; his statement did not have the impact that he had hoped it would.

Once I got home, I read the printout for the class I needed to take. The course was Monday through Friday at a nearby city. Reading further, I saw that the lessons started the following Monday, and of course, it was already Friday. That would give me just the weekend to study before the class. I got busy setting up a space to start reading the big thick book. Upon opening the book, I read in big, bold letters, "Before you schedule your test, you should study these materials for three months." To say I was shocked would be an understatement. I could not believe my eyes. I read that warning repeatedly, each time hoping that I had read it wrong. Unfortunately, I had not. I knew Alistair was aware of this suggestion/warning and must have gotten a chuckle thinking about it.

If he expected me to call him and complain that I needed

more time, he was sorely mistaken. If I am one thing, it is determined and strong-willed, and I never give up.

I spent the entire weekend studying the materials, reading the book from cover to cover. I read it thoroughly three times, trying to remember as much as I could. I attended the course on Monday and was the first to arrive and the last to leave each day. I took copious notes and dried up two highlighters.

I was one determined woman who would not back down, letting that Good Old Boy win.

When I passed the exam, I presented the certificate to Alistair with great pride and enthusiasm. To see the look on his face was priceless: he had been so sure that I would fail; he was upset and speechless. Fighting the urge to say, "I told you so," I politely asked if I could get the materials for the next test. When Alistair finally composed himself, he handed me three more manuals and reminded me that I would need to pass all three of the exams before he could hire me.

Passing all these exams would make me one of the few financial planners to have all those designations. It was not long after that meeting that I returned and presented him three more certificates.

Alistair had no choice now; he had to hire me, and he was not very happy about it.

He gave me several forms to fill out to make it official. While I was signing them, he muttered under his breath that I would not last the year, that I would fail. By then, you know that was not going to happen.

Not only did I finish out the year, but I also ended it with a sales award. Oh, dear, I hope I didn't crush Alistair's ego too much.

CHAPTER 5

Everything I Have Heard about Good Old Boys Is True

My first day on the job was both exciting and intimidating. I didn't know what the future held for me, and I was going to waste no time getting the show on the road. The office manager showed me around the office, giving me a grand tour and, in the end, showed me where my office would be. It was small: a desk chair, two visitor chairs, and a small cabinet. On the desk was a computer and a phone, an actual desk phone, something rarely seen these days. Anything else I needed or wanted, I had to provide myself. It wasn't long before I got my first visitor. Once he came into my office, three more men followed. They were anxious to let me know that they were top producers, that this office only had two women, and that I had just brought that count to three. They wasted no time letting me know that they were in control, and I was to stay out of their way. I was somewhat disappointed that they hadn't brought me a welcome basket.

I soon learned the best way to protect yourself from the Good Old Boys was to stay away from them, and that was just what I did. I kept to myself as much as possible. At first, it seemed to be working. Had I known what I was in for, I might have made my first day my last day. Other than not wanting me there in the first place, the Good Old Boys, for the most part, left me alone. I even made a few friends among them.

I had no experience in the financial business, so I went to every meeting and every available workshop. I was eager to learn as much as I could in as little time as possible. Training managers led the meeting, and it soon became apparent that they required some severe training themselves. None of the three men seemed to know what they were talking about and often disagreed with one another. They were Good Old Boys, for sure. They were unprofessional and lacked morals of any kind. To say their business practices were self-serving is an understatement.

I stopped going to their meetings altogether after one session was a lesson on how to forge a client's signature. They would put a form the client had previously signed on a glass window and then line up a blank application, so the signature lines matched. With the sun shining through the paper, they were able to trace the signature on the clean form. I found this appalling and wanted nothing to do with this type of behavior.

I was assigned to a training manager on my first day with the company. As luck would have it, my training manager was none other than Oswald, the laziest of all the training managers. He was also the ringleader of the corrupt practices' meetings. Teaching the new hires, the trick of copying their clients' signatures was his brainchild. Sadly, he was proud of that accomplishment. Oswald had a mean streak, and he was known to have a quick temper and to be ready to throw a punch or two when an argument was not going his way. Honestly, Oswald scared the dickens out of me. The only way Oswald knew how to talk was in a loud, crude, and demanding way.

During my first year with Oswald acting as my training manager, I learned it was best to avoid him. It was easy to stay away from him because he was so lazy, he never did anything that might be work.

Oswald preferred to have other people do his work, but Oswald still wanted to get paid.

He had an anniversary coming up, and he wanted to give his wife an expensive ring. Of course, Oswald seldom worked and did not have enough money to buy the ring. Knowing about each piece of business I turned in, he knew I was expecting a more substantial than average pay.

Oswald came into my office one day and had the paperwork in his hands from my last appointment. He was putting the applications in front of me while he told me to replace my name with his. Thinking Oswald was insane, and I told him no. If I had changed our names, he would have received the commission instead of me. I had bills to pay and was not giving him my commission. Oswald became irate, telling me I had no other choice. After making it clear what would happen if I didn't, he left the room. Oswald was sure I would do as I was told. When payday came, he went to his mailbox to get his check. Of course, my commission was not paid out to him, as he had expected. Oswald came marching down to my office and was so loud I could hear him coming and quickly locked the door. The wall to my office had glass on both sides of it, and Oswald put his check up to the glass and screamed at me, wanting to know where the money was. He started to bang so loudly on my door that other people in nearby offices came to see what all the commotion was. Oswald's supervisor was among the crowd.

It did not take his supervisor long to figure out what was happening. He told Oswald to see him in his office immediately. Much to my relief, Oswald was no longer my training manager.

When a Good Old Boy has his mind made up that he wants something, he will do anything to get what he wants. His supervisor was also a Good Old Boy, and Oswald was off the hook. He received no consequences for his behavior.

As in most cases, the leader of the office sets the tone and business practices for everyone. That was a problem, as the individual in charge of this office was Arnold, and Arnold had serious issues. Arnold went way beyond the standard practices of most Good Old Boys.

I never felt comfortable around Arnold; he creeped me out. On one occasion, he asked me if my daughter could babysit his children. I did not feel comfortable with that situation and declined on behalf of my daughter. As it turned out, I had made the right decision. Arnold had anger issues and could not control his impulses. It wasn't long after he asked my daughter to babysit that Arnold severely beat his girlfriend, breaking the furniture in the process. His girlfriend dropped the charges and bailed him out. Arnold got away with beating his girlfriend, and he felt he could get away with anything. After all, women are too afraid to press charges, so a little apology and a promise never to do it again were all he needed to do.

For days, Arnold did not come into the office; no one knew

where he was, and it is safe to say nobody cared. The office was much more relaxed, and people were happier when Arnold was out of the office. Just as I was becoming accustomed to this new atmosphere, chaos reigned upon the office. Arnold came to the office that day, for the first time in several days. He walked into the building and went straight to his office without a word. Once in, he locked the door. Something he had never done before. Around an hour later, we heard loud voices and men running down the hallway. Not knowing what was going on, but sure that it was nothing that could be good, I locked the door to my office. As I mentioned, there were two large panels of glass on either side of the door, so I could see a little of what was going on around me. Soon, there was banging on a door, and I heard a loud voice saying, "Give yourself up!" Now I knew this was not going to end well. I looked out my window and could see police cars everywhere. There must have been a dozen police cars, and the men running down the hall were indeed police officers. After hearing another loud knock and the command to "Give yourself up!" again, I heard a loud crash and the sound of wood splintering. The police officers had smashed the door down and were arresting Arnold.

Now that I knew the police had things under control, I felt that it was safe to walk out of my office. Just as I did, I saw two beefy police officers escorting Arnold down the hall. He was very disheveled and in handcuffs. I will never forget the look in his eye when he saw me. It chilled me to the bone. All I could think of was, *Thank God I didn't let my daughter babysit for this monster.*

We soon learned the charges for Arnold's arrest were rape and attempted murder. It was time for me to start looking for a better job. I now had two years of experience and sales awards to my credit. My education would no longer be an issue. Or so I thought.

CHAPTER 6

My Husband Makes the Coffee at Our House

Just because you are working for a different company doesn't mean you have escaped the Good Old Boys. It only means you are now dealing with a whole new batch of Good Old Boys.

It turned out this new batch of Good Old Boys was worse in many ways. A more significant percentage of the male population was Good Old Boys at this firm. The community of women was much smaller in the region where I worked, and I was the only woman in the area when I started.

At first, that didn't seem to be an issue, unlike at the first company, which was a large office with individual offices inside of it. The conference room, lunchroom, and copy room were all community areas. This setup allowed plenty of time to interface with the Good Old Boys. You could not avoid a run-in with one or another of the Good Old Boys.

While the new firm used individual storefront offices for each of the financial planners, each office had a receptionist and an office manager along with one financial planner. This situation seemed like a dream come true. The only contact I would have with the Good Old Boys would be at regional meetings, and those were just once a month. I quickly settled in and started to grow my business. One day, much to my surprise, three of the men I had worked with at the first company came by to pay a visit. They were interested in how I was doing at this new firm. They also wanted to check out the office and ask some questions. All three of them liked what they saw and were intent on working for this firm. They expected me to set them up with interviews and give them good recommendations. Although they had always been friendly, I didn't know them well. I called the home office and did what I could to ensure that they would get hired.

When I interviewed for my current job, I received a $60,000.00 signing bonus. I received the cash incentive because I had done exceptionally well in my previous position.

All three of these men joined the company and received signing bonuses. The three men all had mediocre performances at the previous firm. I had done a much more impressive job and ranked higher in the statistics than they did. When I heard that their signing bonus was much higher than what I had received, I was devastated. That seemed most unfair until I remembered that as men, they received priority.

After working with this company for a short time, it became apparent that these Good Old Boys did not want to work with a woman. Soon things started to get very nasty. And the situation became worse after I won their coveted trophy at the annual meeting.

Every year at their annual meeting, which everyone across the country attended, they had a contest that everyone competed in, and the Good Old Boys became very competitive. The competition consisted of giving a sales presentation to a panel of unbiased judges from outside the firm. Each year, the trophy was won by one of the seasoned advisers. On the first day of the meeting, there was a lot of trash talk, as several men were confident that they would win this year. The contenders for the trophy were a small group of men who all thought they were the alpha male.

There was a banquet at the end of the week where they announced the winner of the competition. I was surprised at how much this meant to some of these Good Old Boys. Presenting the trophy was held off until after the meal, making it more dramatic. I never gave it much thought. Being a woman with less than one year with the company, I knew it would never be me.

When I heard my name announced as that year's winner of the sales competition, no one was more surprised than I was. I was excited that I had won, and at the same time, I didn't want all the attention that came with it. I made my way to the stage, where the trophy was waiting for me. The president of the company was holding it. The first thing I noticed about the cup was that it was very tall and ornate. Then my attention was drawn to the top of it: there stood a gold-colored man in a suit, holding a gold-colored briefcase. No one thought a woman might be winning this, but one did, and it would have been nice if they had chosen something else to put atop the trophy.

There was a loud sound of chattering and grumbling coming from the audience. One Good Old Boy was more emphatic than all the others, and he shouted out, "No woman should ever get

this trophy! That's why there is a man atop and not a woman!"
After accepting the trophy, I quickly left the stage and kept
on walking until I was out of the auditorium and safely in the
women's bathroom. Once in the privacy of the women's room,
I began to sob. Not wanting even one Good Old Boy to see me
cry, I went straight up to my hotel room. I did not attend the
meeting the next morning, I avoided everyone associated with
the company and left on an early flight.

After that meeting, I was on the radar of the Good Old Boys,
who set out to make my life miserable. At least they were good at
that one thing because I sure was unhappy with all their antics.
If they had put as much effort into their career as they did their
attempts to sabotage me, they just might have been successful.
The Good Old Boys went out of their way to come up with
different ways to make my job difficult. If they could embarrass
me, so much the better. The Good Old Boys tried every trick
in the book to make me cry. They were never successful in that
endeavor. My number one rule was "Never let them see you cry."
It was clear that they had the full support of upper management,
which allowed them to do whatever they wanted, making it
useless to complain.

The next hurdle I had to overcome was a very sinister plot,
one that I did not see coming. I received a notice that a new hire
was coming to my office the following Monday, and I needed to
make sure I was in my office for the entire day so I could show
him the ropes. What they forgot to tell me was that he would
be staying the whole week. He came on appointments with me,
watched, took notes, and asked a million questions while observ-
ing me put together a portfolio. He was very annoying. Although
he had to ask many questions, he was a know-it-all and tried to

tell me that what I was doing was all wrong. A person can only take so much of this. By the third day, I told him there would be no criticizing me, period. If he felt I was doing it wrong, he was free to leave at any time. That was a very long week; I did not get everything done that I wanted to. I was so glad to see him leave on Friday. If I had wanted to be a trainer, I would have applied for the job.

My happiness did not last long; the next Monday, another new hire came through my door. This time, I had no warning, he just showed up. He also stayed for the week. If possible, he was more arrogant and annoying than the first guy.

Every Monday morning, a new person would walk through my door. Each one would stay a week, and these Good Old Boys just got worse as time progressed. I called someone in upper management to ask if they would kindly stop sending their new hires to my office. My request fell on deaf ears, and another Good Old Boy showed up the very next Monday. Being prepared to take matters into my own hands when this Old Boy said he was there for training, I pulled up my big girl panties and sent him packing. Within the hour, my phone rang. It was the same Good Old Boy I had spoken to earlier, the one I asked to stop sending me new hires. This Good Old Boy was angry; he had not gotten his way, and he did not like that. The fact that a woman had disobeyed his wishes was more than he could handle. He became verbally abusive, using some choice words, a few that I had not heard before, nor do I care to hear again.

I sat and listened while he raged on, holding back laughter because he was no longer making sense. When he had blown off an incredible amount of steam and finally stopped talking, it was my turn to speak; I felt no need to apologize or defend myself.

I told this nasty-mouthed Good Old Boy that I had carefully read my contract and found that nowhere was it written that I had to train other advisers. I reminded him that they had people on staff who did their training for them and received compensation for doing so. Unless he wanted to pay me the same pay rate, I would no longer accommodate them. The poor Good Old Boy was left stuttering and stammering. He was beside himself. A woman had never told him no and stood up to him, defending herself. It was beyond his comprehension that something like this could happen to him. He learned a lesson that day, an experience that he would always remember. He found out that women do have a voice, and some women are not afraid to use it. Nobody had warned him that this might happen. I hoped that he would be more respectful of women in the future. The sad reality is that he most likely continued with the same behavior.

The only way to survive in a man's world is to stand up for yourself and never show any signs of weakness. Always be confident and challenge anyone who is treating you with anything other than respect.

While working for this latest company, word got out that I did not have a college degree. My lack of a degree amused the Good Old Boys until they realized that I was doing as well as they were and, in some cases, even better. It suddenly was no longer funny; it was an embarrassment to some. The idea that a woman could keep up with them and do it without having a college degree was a double loss to their pride.

While attending a meeting with a large attendance, one smart-ass addressed me with a question. "How do you expect to compete with men like myself when I have several degrees, and you have no degree?"

My quick comeback was "Pretty darn well if I do say so myself."

Silence filled the room; suddenly, all eyes were on me. I am sure that they all expected me to cry, while some wanted to watch me squirm. These Good Old Boys were vicious, and if I didn't stand up to them right then and put them in their place, things would only get worse.

I spoke with bold confidence when I told him, "I think you are out of line, and I will tell you why I think so. My numbers speak for themselves. Have you not noticed that I am consistently one of the top producers in this region? While you all have a degree or two and I have, as you so rudely pointed out, none, I would also like to point out to you that I have no student loans. Can you say the same?"

I had so much more to say to this arrogant, chauvinistic fool; I commenced firing questions at him. It was like lobbing baseballs at him; everyone was a direct hit. The silence had now turned into giggles, and this time, it was not directed at me. Since it was this Good Old Boy who had made such an issue of my lack of a college degree, it was the perfect lead into the final question. "Just how does it feel knowing that a woman, no less one without a college degree, manages to surpass you in production?"

Because a handful of men in the audience were not Good Old Boys, I did not want them to think I lumped them all into one category. I took the time to thank the men who were kind, courteous, and respectful; I told them they knew who they were, and I had the utmost respect for them, unlike the sanctimonious Good Old Boys. I did not include the gentlemen in the room as part of the circus with the other baboons, the men I called Good Old Boys.

It was because of this meeting that I decided to pursue my college degree. I would be doing this for myself and no other reason. I was already well-established as a financial adviser, and it would not mean I would make more money. The idea of attending a university to take classes was out of the question since I worked so many hours and was also raising two children. I found a university that offered online courses, which also accepted life experience and the many credits I had received taking classes for continued education. I had already accumulated several credit hours toward my degree, and it didn't take long at all before I earned my Bachelor of Science degree in finance. I am glad I did this. It gave me a great sense of accomplishment, even if it took me so many years to complete.

That memorable meeting made me think hard about my future and the goals I wanted to attain. I concluded that my goals could not come to fruition there. It was time to find a better match. I needed a company that would support me, not attempt to suppress me.

One thing I did learn while working for this company is that there are Good Old Boys everywhere you go; you can't avoid them. Instead, you need to be confident, never show fear, and set up ground rules regarding respect and what behaviors you will and will not accept.

It helps to keep in mind that there will be different rules and expectations for men and women. This practice is not fair, nor is it legal, but it is reality. Do your best, never give up, and never put up with bad behavior of any kind.

CHAPTER 7

The Angry Man

While the work environment seems to be the area in which the Good Old Boys are more noticeable, their playground is much more expansive than just where they work. Some Good Old Boys who have been a card-carrying member for most of their lives carry the chauvinistic behavior wherever they go and into whatever they are doing. They act like Good Old Boys while shopping, at events they attend, even while at church. If you were to think about the male members of your church or place of worship, it shouldn't take you long to come up with a few names of Good Old Boys. You may not have had an opportunity to observe them; you still know they are Good Old Boys just by watching their attitude. Remember, they are everywhere, around every corner, behind every door, and it is not hard to identify them.

If you interact with your neighbors, you will observe them in their natural environment. Human nature shows us that we have one personality that we show to others when we are at work and a different character when we are at home. The change occurs naturally; it seldom is done on purpose. In most cases, their bad behavior is much worse when the Good Old Boys are in their home environment. This behavior, to some extent, is like having home advantage for athletics.

To prove that not all of my experiences with Good Old Boys occurred only in the work environment, I will relate a story that happened to me while driving my car, delivering free papers to entire neighborhoods in the middle of the night. This interaction occurred over thirty years ago, which also shows that I was no stranger to the Good Old Boys when I started to work in the financial world.

Many years ago, before I became a financial planner, my husband and I had a motor paper route. We covered several subdivisions, delivering the free paper that came out once a week. We each drove separate cars and split the territory between us. We stayed with the same routine every week. That way, we always knew where the other one was. We would cross paths a couple of times so that we knew the other one was safe. During this time, there were no cell phones; we were in the days of the pager. Having a pager was of no use to us because a phone was still necessary to send the message. After working at this job for a while, we bought walkie-talkies. The area we were delivering in was dark, with no streetlights. Occasionally, we could see a porch light or spotlights on top of a garage. The new motion sensor lights had just appeared on the market, and as luck would have it, there were a lot of people buying them. Driving up to a driveway and having a light automatically come on was a blessing. It helped us to see where we were throwing the paper, which significantly reduced the number of newspapers landing in the bushes.

The reason we decided to do this was twofold: it paid a lot of money for working one night a week, and because it was during the night, we could also work our day jobs.

It soon became a comfortable routine, and the extra money was beneficial. I was able to save enough to pursue my new career. I would be able to attend classes and not have to worry about income loss. What could go wrong? A question you should never ask. Every time I did, I found out, and it was never a favorable ending. This time was no different.

The evening started just fine; there was a full moon that provided extra light, and that was always a plus. I was about halfway through my route, which made it around 1:30 a.m. I was ahead of schedule, which doesn't happen often. I was in good spirits, knowing I would be done early and might get a little extra sleep before I had to start my day job.

I pulled up to a house just as I had done for months before that night. When I stopped, I reached over to my passenger's seat to grab a newspaper rolled tightly in a plastic bag. As my back faced my open window, a man jumped out from behind a large bush. He approached my window and put a gun to my head. He was angry and smelled like alcohol. He demanded to know why I kept leaving a newspaper in his driveway when he did not want one. Seeing that he was unsteady on his feet, I put the car in drive and pushed that gas pedal down as hard as I could. As I sped away, he jumped into his car, sitting right there in the driveway. He was following me and was also driving fast. I grabbed my walkie-talkie and was thankful My husband responded immediately. Trying to escape from this angry man and holding the cumbersome walkie-talkie was difficult. Mike asked where I was and quickly started to direct me to his location. There was just one problem with his instructions or my ability to follow them. I drove myself right into a dead end. I was trapped. My pursuer stopped his car and got out with a gun in hand, quickly approaching my window. The window was no longer down, and I had locked the car, but I do not think that would have been a deterrent to a gunshot. Just as I was sure I was going to die right there in my car, I heard a loud crash. My husband had caught up to me and saw the man approaching my window. To distract him, my husband crashed into his parked car. The commotion alerted the neighbors, and now a neighbor was calling the police. Although very damaged, his car was still able to be driven, and the man left in a hurry.

I assume that the reason he left was to get rid of his gun because he was only gone a few minutes and returned, arriving just before the police officers came. There were two squad cars, each with two police officers in them and an EMS vehicle on the scene. Sirens blaring and lights flashing, it felt as if we were filming for the television show *COPS*.

As the police officers escorted us to the squad cars, one for each myself, my husband, and the angry man, a fourth police officer was questioning the neighbors. They were trying to ascertain what had happened and who the bad guy in this situation was. It didn't take long to conclude that the angry man was the bad guy. The angry man was given a free ride to the police station, while the paramedics were making sure that neither my husband nor I were hurt.

If I came to the station the next day to give my statement, we were free to go. That was enough excitement for one night.

We went straight home and did not finish our routes. We also never delivered another newspaper again.

The next day, I went into the police station to give my statement. I had never been inside a police station before and was nervous. My husband came along for moral support. When I walked into the interview room, there sat an officer who looked just like Eddie Murphy. Now, who can be frightened by Eddie Murphy?

The first words out of the officer's mouth were, "Now that is taking not wanting a newspaper way too far." I had to agree; he could have called the newspaper company and asked to be on the list not to receive a paper. There was already a dozen or so names on the list, and we were careful not to give any of them a paper.

When they questioned the angry man, he told the officer that he had called the newspaper office three times to tell them he did not want the paper. After checking with the newspaper office, where they learned that he had not called at all, the officer proceeded to charge him with several offenses. One of the charges was an unlawful use of a gun and pursuing me with the intent to harm. Those are the only two that stuck, but he was in some serious trouble. The angry man also tried to pursue charges against my husband for damage to his car. The officer wanted to teach this guy a lesson. He did not charge my husband with anything and did not write up a report of the crash. Instead, he did write the angry man a citation for parking in the street and obstructing traffic. That one stuck also.

I learned a lesson that night. I learned that Good Old Boys, alcohol, and guns do not mix. When a Good Old Boy is drinking and gets agitated, avoid him at all costs. Just as I was not able to know that an angry man would be waiting for me in the bushes, you will not always know when you are dealing with a Good Old Boy; the trick is to understand how to protect yourself once you encounter an out-of-control Good Old Boy.

CHAPTER 8

Women Can Make Decisions Too

The Good Old Boys are everywhere; sometimes, it feels as if they are lurking around every corner. No matter where you go, there they are.

Because they are everywhere, you should never attempt to make a significant purchase alone. Always have a male with you, not necessarily to speak or even interact with the salesman. His presence alone will deflect some, if not all, of the chauvinistic Good Old Boys from being Good Old Boys. When Good Old Boys see a woman walk through the door, they immediately recognize her as a target. They think that all women are putty in their hands; what you need to do is show them how wrong they are. You need to stop the Good Old Boy before he gets started. Tell him that you have researched the product that you are interested in, and you do not need his help now. Tell the Good Old

Boy that you will summon him when his assistance is required. That tells him upfront that you are in control, and you are confident enough to make your own choices. If the Good Old Boy is so ignorant that he keeps bothering you, look him in the eye and repeat what you told him when you walked in. Follow that up by telling him if he cannot conform to your wishes, you will speak with his boss. If that doesn't work, I am sure you will want to punch him in the face, but don't do that. It is called assault and battery. Since you can't do that, you should walk out of the door and take your business elsewhere.

I find it strange that most sales staff for household appliances are men. I would think that a woman would be better suited for the job. But then again, I am old school. I must remind myself that men cook and clean almost as much as women. I know that my husband cleans, cooks, and shops for groceries. He doesn't do all of it, but he certainly helps.

Not too long ago, my husband and I went to one of the big box stores where you can buy everything from food, clothes, tools, and cleaning supplies to appliances. We were in the market for a linen closet, one that is freestanding. My husband and I both went to make the purchase. I was designing the bathroom and knew just what we wanted. We discussed it before we went to the store and agreed. We looked at what they had available and found one that would come close to our specifications. When a salesman approached us, I told him we were interested in ordering that cabinet, and we would need it to be customized to fit our specifications. I looked the man in the eye when I spoke, and my husband said nothing. Immediately, it was clear that we were dealing with a Good Old Boy because the salesman completely ignored me and what I had said and turned to my husband to ask him what size we were looking to purchase. My husband is accustomed to this Good Old Boy attitude and just smiled and said that his wife would give him the information. The Good Old Boy continued to address my husband and ignore me. After a few minutes of this banter, I spoke up rather loudly and told him that I would be making all the decisions, and he needed to communicate with me directly.

My husband smiled and asked the Old Boy, "Is that going to work for you?" When he did not answer, my husband told him that we would go to another store if he could not treat me with respect. Our purchase was well over a thousand dollars, and apparently, he was working on a commission basis, because he quickly said, "Okay, no problem." Sometimes even with a man present, a Good Old Boy will still act like a pompous ass.

I found out firsthand that going to buy a large ticket item alone becomes a nightmare if you do not take control from the beginning. Car salespeople, for example, work on a commission basis; the more significant the sale, the bigger the commission. You would think that the prospect of an enormous payday would be incentive enough to treat all potential customers with respect. Oddly enough, in some cases, it isn't. It appears that many of the Good Old Boys are unable to control themselves long enough to overlook the fact that they are dealing with a woman. It might be their ego, driving them to act in such a chauvinistic manner. The prospect of a hefty commission is not enough for these Good Old Boys to treat women as they treat men.

I feel confident that the Good Old Boys treat women this way even if the commission is small or there is no commission at all. It is pathetic.

Take, for example, a woman by herself who takes her car into the shop for a minor repair and is told that she needs to have hundreds of dollars in other maintenance repairs. Most likely, they will say to her that if she does not have these repairs done, it will not be safe to drive her car. Because she is now frightened and knows nothing about cars, she agrees and is given a bill for much more than necessary. The mechanic took advantage of her because he knew she would not question him. What a shame, and to think this happens every day across the country. Of course, we can't assume that all service repairmen are Good Old Boys or that they take advantage of unsuspecting women. Some servicemen do not treat women that way. Instead, they go beyond the call of duty, once they know the woman is single or especially if she is elderly. My daughter was a single mother. When she had car problems, there was a mechanic down the street who would give her discounts and sometimes not charge her at all. She paid him back with numerous recommendations. It worked well for both.

Today, many women have become independent, with or without a man in their life. In a couple when both partners work, there often is no time for the husband to accompany the woman while making a significant purchase, and this should not be necessary. We still have the stigma that men should make all the decisions, and men should hold jobs with authority. Maybe someday this will change, but I won't be holding my breath.

While I was working as a financial adviser, frequently, people would come into my office, passing through a big glass door that had my name in large letters on it. It also listed me as the financial adviser, along with my designations. Once inside, they asked if they could speak to my guy, the actual financial adviser. Although the door had my name on it, and there were several framed certificates hanging on the wall, each with my name on it, some people would still ask to speak to "my guy." These people could not comprehend that a woman could hold the position of a financial adviser. They assumed it had to be a man, and I had to be the secretary. Instead of getting upset, I would smile and tell them that I did not have a guy, but it might be a good idea for me to hire a guy to be my secretary. Nervous laughter would follow that statement until it finally sank in that I was the guy that they were asking to see. I never did hire a guy to be my secretary, but it might have been a good idea.

I do not enjoy shopping for a new car. I am not a car person. To me, a car is just transportation and, in my case, my office on wheels. When it came time to purchase a new car, I started to do extensive research months before I was ready to buy. I wanted to make sure to choose the right one because I would have it a long time and spend many hours in it while working. I compared features, gas mileage, reliability, and of course, what *Consumer Report* had to say about each possibility. Once I had made my graphs, and comparisons, I settled on a Lincoln. They rated highest with *Consumer Report*, and it was a comfortable car and had a history of lasting a long time. I went to the website of the local Lincoln dealership, where I chose the color and the options I wanted. With this information, I was ready to go and buy it. With my printout in hand and my checkbook in my pocket, I was off to the friendly Lincoln dealership.

It was not busy at the dealership: it was midday and a Monday, not a popular time to buy a car. While I parked my car, I could see that there were no customers in the showroom. I was sure this would be quick and easy. I could not have been more wrong. Walking in, I saw that three men were standing by one of the cubicles, deep in conversation. They all ignored me; I walked around the cars in the showroom. I still was not offered any help. When I saw that they were not going to assist me, I asked them as a whole, "Can someone please help me?" They all looked at each other before one reluctantly said he would help me—not that he would be happy to help me, just that he would help me. At least it was a start.

Now that I had the assistance of a salesman, I began to tell him that I wanted to order a car and showed him the printout I had made, with the details of all the options that I had chosen. I asked him how long it would take for the car to be delivered. He handed me back my printout and told me to come back when my husband was with me, as he didn't have any time to waste. I was stunned and asked him if he just told me to leave and come back with my husband. I could not believe he could be so rude and condescending, but he could. He said to me, "That is what I told you; your husband will have to be here. You will not be able to make such a big decision without him here."

It took every ounce of strength I had to refrain from punching him in the nose and screaming profanities. Keeping my composure, I politely asked if I could speak to his manager or possibly the owner of the dealership. Taking the salesman off guard, he asked me why I would want to talk to the boss. I must have been talking much louder than I realized, because a much older man in a very costly designer suit walked into the showroom and asked if there was a problem. I reached out and shook his hand, telling him who I was. Of course, he didn't know me from Adam, but it was a formality, and I wanted to conduct myself like the professional that I am. After telling him my name, I went on to say, "I will tell you what the problem is:

your salesmen are chauvinistic and pompous fools." I showed
him the printout of the car I was there to purchase and asked
him how much the Good Old Boy had just lost in commissions
and how much money he had cost the dealership by losing this
sale. I went on to tell him that I made my own money and my
own decisions, and I did not need my husband's permission to
buy a car. I had come with my checkbook ready to buy the car,
and he had told me to go home and get my husband because he
didn't have time to waste.

I concluded by saying that the staff all needed a lesson in
manners and how to treat women and to have a good day. I left
and never went back. I didn't even buy a Lincoln after that bad
experience. I am sure not all Lincoln dealerships have salesmen
who are so rude. I was just turned off by Lincolns altogether
after that.

That salesman was a die-hard Good Old Boy, who had zero
respect for women, so much so that he didn't want to be both-
ered by them. His attitude cost him a lot of money that day, but
I doubt that he learned a lesson, and I suspect he still behaves the
same way today. Have you ever heard the phrase "You can't teach
an old dog new tricks"? I believe that it is easier to nail Jell-O to
a tree than it is to change a Good Old Boy's habits.

CHAPTER 9

Boys Will Be Boys

After working with two different financial firms and having bad experiences with Good Old Boys at each one, I knew they would be wherever I went. Changing firms does not eliminate your exposure to Good Old Boys; there will be new Good Old Boys at the next firm. I had to figure out what my next move would be, and I hoped it would be my last move.

Part of the problem is that most firms are dominated by males, with few, if any, women. I had chosen to be in this business, I had a financial degree, and I enjoyed the job. The only problem was the Good Old Boys I had to work with made my life miserable. They drained me emotionally and consumed too much time (fending them off). I did a little research on what kind of occupations were available and found there were several options. One of the options that intrigued me was working at a bank. That had never occurred to me. It sounded like a perfect solution. Banks generally were known to have women be the majority rather than the minority of their personnel. I set about finding a bank in my area that was hiring financial advisers. Banks were just starting to have financial advisers on their staff. It was still a relatively new practice, so I didn't expect that there would be too many possibilities.

I began a search for a bank that was adding financial advisers to their platform. Surprisingly, it didn't take long. The bank I chose was starting their financial adviser platform and had not rolled it out yet. At first, I thought it would be an excellent opportunity to be part of the program from the start. The issue was, they didn't know what they were doing, having never done it before. It became clear, almost immediately, that they were learning as they went. That was not for me. I wanted to be off and running and not go through the slow and painful growing pains. I didn't have trouble signing up new clients and helping them with their portfolios, because I had experience working as a financial adviser. I found it rather easy and was accumulating many clients whom I sold financial products to, which translated into a nice paycheck. The bank only paid the financial advisers once a month, which was a challenge to the budget. The first month I didn't have much of an opportunity to work with the clients. Therefore, I received a small paycheck, but the next month, I was able to see several more clients, and with the amount I expected to receive for my next payday, it was starting to look promising.

When that day came, I was disappointed to see how small my paycheck was considering all the work I had done. The excuse I received was they were learning as they went. They also had to set up their system to be able to distribute the commissions to the adviser. Currently, the commissions all went directly to the bank. It then became the responsibility of the bank manager to break them down and distribute to the advisers what they had earned. This practice was not an acceptable system at all. The manager never understood how to do it and was extremely upset when my paycheck was more substantial than hers for one month. Because they were learning as they went, the bank was also making changes—all for their benefit. Soon, they were doing whatever they wanted with no consideration of the original contract I had signed. Looking it over more carefully, I found that it was ambiguous at best. According to the agreement, they were not breaking any of the terms since these were open for debate. There was no way I was going to continue to work under these circumstances.

Odd that this behavior crossed over to the women "superiors." They all acted in the same manner as the Good Old Boys. My trust in all humanity had flown right out of the window. That is the reason I am opposed to women acting like men to get the job done, but then, no one asked for my opinion now did they.

It was time to update my résumé. I would have to put up with Good Old Boys wherever I went, but at least I knew what to expect, and that is half of the battle.

The next stop on my search for suitable employment was a Fortune 500 Company. It seemed ideal, but I had fallen for that in the past. I had experience in financial planning and in dealing with Good old Boys, and my new attitude was *bringing it on*.

It did not take long to discover that I had landed amid the worst of the worst. These men were card-holding members of the Good Old Boys' Club, and they didn't try to hide it. They had honed their ability to be bullies, chauvinists, tyrants, and some words that my grandma told me never to use in public.

These Good Old Boys had each other covered no matter what, and there was no limit to their nasty deeds. It is most unfortunate that I spent the majority of my career in this house of horrors.

I can read people well and spot the red flags they throw out, and I should have left when I saw the first red flag. It wasn't the first red flag that I missed. There were several, but wanting to see the good in people, I ignored the red flags. Call it denial, or maybe I didn't want to start over again. Besides, what was the point? The Good Old Boys would be waiting for me everywhere I went, and I was getting too old to change jobs again.

Not all men are the same; many are gentlemen who treat women with respect. The only problem is gentlemen are few and far between. It takes skill to sort them out and know who a gentleman is and who is a Good Old Boy. You don't have to labor over this for too long; the Good Old Boys show who they are quickly.

I missed my first red flag during my interview when asked if I planned to have more children. Even back then, it was not legal to ask that question. What he was asking me was "Will you be taking time off work to bring a new life into this world?"—a question not asked to men. Now we see more men helping raise children, and there are househusbands as well as housewives.

If my interview didn't scare me off, this next experience should have done the trick. It was horrible, humiliating, and demeaning. Since our jobs involved traveling to our clients, to see them at their sites, a Good Old Boy named Spike had the task of taking me with him the next day on a ride-along so that

I could shadow him. The only information Spike received was that I was a female a few years younger than he was. Although the district had many advisers, there were only four who were female.

Spike arrived at the office the next day, eager to meet the new adviser he would be spending the day with, showing her the ropes. When the manager introduced me to Spike, he was visibly disappointed. As it turns out, although not bad looking—I am a bit overweight—I was not at all what Spike had envisioned.

Spike abruptly headed for the door and told me over his shoulder, "You had better be able to keep up with me." When we got to the parking lot, I saw that he had one of those expensive sports cars, of the type that sat very low to the ground. Getting into this car would be easy, getting out, not so much. Getting out of a vehicle that sits so low to the ground is difficult because I have weak muscles.

Not only did he not open the door for me, but he also snarled at me, "You're on your own. Good luck." To say it was a quiet drive and a very long day would be sugarcoating the situation. If this was how these Good Old Boys welcomed me to the new company, I dreaded to think about what lay ahead. Being treated this way on my first day should also have been a red flag. Now I had missed two red flags.

There were many positive aspects to this job. I won several awards, trips, and trophies. I also got to meet many cherished clients who are still friends to this day. But working for this company was so stressful, it began to take a toll on my health. The everyday stress was exhausting, and the frequent crises brought on by deception, lies, and the nasty behavior of the Good Old Boys had caused me to dread going into the office. It was a situation where I loved what I was doing; it was the people I had to work with that caused me angst.

It was always open season on women, and the Good Old Boys took their shots and were sometimes even praised for doing so. They were an evil group of boys, worse than any of the others I had ever known. I never knew what corner they were lurking behind.

My job at this company was to work with nonprofit clients, helping them invest in their 403B retirement plans. This group consisted mostly of teachers and hospital employees, as well as a few small for-profit companies. When I began to work for them, I received a book of business, which was three school districts that included everyone who already had an account with us. It became my job to sign up new clients, increase the amount the old clients were contributing, and, when they retired, develop a retirement plan for them. The book of business was the heartbeat of the job. The more extensive the client base in your book, the more money you made and the bigger the opportunity to increase the book and your income.

Dexter was devious; he was also passive-aggressive, and that is a lousy combination for a Good Old Boy. Dexter was very blatant when it came to his misdeeds. He was abusive and almost seemed proud of it. Some of the words that came spewing out of his mouth were outrageous. Dexter had no conscience and no filter. He made sure that I knew he favored sexy young women, at the same time making crude remarks to me just to tell me that I was neither young nor sexy. I thought it was most inappropriate, and yet somehow, Dexter always got away with it. I had no desire to be attractive in his eyes. I had a job to do, I knew how to dress for business, and as far as my age, it was just a number. Dexter continued to make crude remarks regarding my looks or what I was wearing. Dexter just said anything that was a put-down; he did not hold back.

I was hoping once I had learned the ropes and started to become a well-established adviser, he would back down. Sadly, that never happened. I just ignored him and didn't let it bother me and that seemed to upset him more. I also noticed that he became irate when I started to outperform his Good Old Boys. His secretary overheard him telling his boys that they needed to do whatever it took to exceed me in the numbers game and assured them they would have his full support. Of course, his boys were not very good at what they did, and on top of that, they were lazy. I was not an expert; nor was I a genius. I simply worked harder and longer. Any of them could have improved their numbers if they had worked every day.

The company had a steadfast rule: no one was to solicit or any way to try to take clients away from your book. From the best I could tell, everyone honored that rule. But, of course, I was wrong. I soon learned that Dexter's secretary had taken a group of my clients and set them up in a way that a Good Old Boy got paid for them, but my name was listed when they needed any unpaid service. When I brought this to Dexter's attention, he attempted to shame me by telling me I was petty and heartless, that his Good Old Boy who was getting paid for work that I did lived in a remote area and didn't have enough clients to give him enough income. He had three little kids, and if I demanded that these clients be put back in my name so I could get paid for the work I was already doing, I would be taking food from the little kids because their dad would not make enough to feed them. This tactic was a whole new way of Good Old Boys suppressing women that I had never encountered. Doing business this way was stealing from me and giving it to a Good Old Boy, another way for the club to take care of each other. I was not about to let anyone bully me by using guilt. I informed Dexter that he needed to pay me for the work I did and not give the pay to his Good Old Boy.

As time went on, my success was mounting; my numbers were now on the top of the list. That made me a top producer. However, I did not know this until one day I was talking to his secretary, and she told me that she thought it was disgusting how Dexter treated me. Since I was a top producer, he should respect me. This statement took me by surprise. I knew he treated me terribly, but I had not realized I was a top producer and told her as much. I am not one to follow my progress and that of others, so I had no idea when the secretary pulled out the reports and showed me that my name was consistently in the top three advisers of the region. I was stunned; no one had ever shared this with me.

The regional managers each received their advisers' overall progress with the top three in the nation highlighted. The regional vice president is praised for the excellent work of his best three advisers and told to let the advisers know they are top producers for the month and to give them kudos for a job well done. Dexter had never said a word to me, and I had been in the top three for almost a year. At local meetings, he would praise the other two on the list but never mention my name. Knowing that my success made Dexter irate was all I needed to try harder.

Good Old Boys do not like to acknowledge the success of a woman. They are in denial that a woman could even do a good job. It hurts their pride to have a woman do well, which is stupid if you think about it. I would think that men would find some twisted way of believing that a woman could only be successful because a man had made her successful. We will keep that idea under our hat and be thankful that it is not happening.

As Dexter kept a sharp eye on the progress of his Good Old Boys, he was disappointed to see that their numbers stayed the same or went down. This situation had Dexter so frustrated he decided to take matters into his own hands and started to methodically transfer clients from my name to that of one of his boys. With more clients came more opportunities, and his boys would be able to increase their production with these added clients. It seemed like the perfect strategy. Dexter underestimated the laziness of all his boys. Just because they had more clients to work with did not mean they would work. *Work* was a dirty word for these lame-brained idiots. Their boss could spoon-feed them any way he wanted, and there would always be one missing element, and that is ambition. Dexter had a plan to knock down my production and build up the business of his boys. It did not work. Even with fewer clients, I still increased my output. Dexter's plan to undermine me blew up in his face. He underestimated my moxie.

Dexter's next plan was even better in his view. He assigned me to a new territory, knowing that I would have to work hard to build it up. I did just that. I started a well-thought-out marketing campaign. I reached out to all the current clients with letters and phone calls. I began to set up appointments, filling the next few weeks with meetings. I had this under control and was happy yet suspicious that Dexter had assigned me this new district. Just as I had anticipated, I received a phone call from the house of hell. I was being summoned to Dexter's office and told to be there within the hour. A feeling of dread came over me. I knew nothing good would come from this meeting, and I was right. Dexter wasted no time and got right to the point. He informed me that he was taking my new territory away from me and giving it to Arnold. He thought Arnold was better suited for that area, and the clients were now in Arnold's name. Dexter asked me if I had contacted all these new clients or possibly set up appointments. I told him that I had done just that, thinking he would let me continue. I was speechless when he said to me that any meetings that I had made should go to Arnold immediately.

Dexter was an a##, but why did I not see this coming? After all, I knew how the Good Old Boy operated. It was not fair, and there was nothing I could do about it. I had spent many hours and several hundred dollars of my money marketing to this group. When I voiced this concern to Dexter, he just laughed at me. It was all for nothing. Now Arnold was all set and just had to show up for the meetings. I voiced my concern to Dexter and asked him how he would replace my loss. He smirked and said, "I will think about that and get back to you." No surprise, he never did get back to me, and Arnold never followed up on any of the leads and did not show up for most of the appointments. All of this was a loss to the company. None of that concerned Dexter. He was too busy plotting his next scheme.

I was furious, yet I knew I needed to make the best of the situation, and I certainly was not going to cry in front of him or show any emotion. I would get even, but it would be on my terms and on my time frame.

I would become more successful, knowing this would piss him off. In the meantime, I had to be vigilant and watch my back. Who knew what dirty deed he had up his sleeve? Not long after this fiasco, I noticed my client list was beginning to diminish rapidly. I realized that Dexter was behind it again. Dexter was not going to give up. Imagine what he could have accomplished if he had spent all that negative energy on something worthwhile.

CHAPTER 10

Why Are Men So Dogmatic?

*D*ogmatic is a perfect word to describe Good Old Boys. It represents a Good old Boy better than any other word in the English language, covering so many of their behaviors all in one word. Dogmatic describes a person characterized by an authoritative, arrogant assertion of unproved or unprovable principles. That sounds about right from what I have experienced. There is a long list of descriptive words for dogmatic men. They include *emphatic, imperative, authoritative, domineering, arrogant, overbearing, pushy, opinionated, bigoted, racist, biased, one-sided, narrow-minded*, intolerant, and finally, *fanatical*. Every one of these words fits the description of a Good Old Boy. While a single Good Old Boy will not necessarily exhibit all these behaviors, each Good Old Boy will display a few, and even just one is one too many.

Dexter is an excellent example of a Good Old Boy displaying a multitude of these behaviors, which is most likely why he was the leader of the pack. Dexter had created a tight-knit group of men, all having the same objective: to keep that glass ceiling intact and more durable than ever. Their motto was no women allowed unless they were serving coffee. Good Old Boys think women are there to help them and not to be their equal. Such a thought, they must know that this is 2019 and not medieval times.

The question remains, why are men so dogmatic? One of the many arguments could be how their parents raised them, or possibly their birth order. Another possibility is that a single parent raised them. Whatever the excuse, the Good Old Boys are a difficult group to deal with; that is for sure.

If you go way back to when God created Adam and Eve, the fact that God created Eve with a rib from Adam might signify Adam's dominance over Eve. Men have carried that feeling of dominance ever since that time.

Any way you choose to look at it, men have remained in control, and women are still struggling to do more in the boardroom than serve coffee. This obstacle is very daunting, and because of it, women must work twice as hard as men, often for less pay. This frustration is impossible, and the Good Old Boys will continue to hire and promote men who reflect the same ideals as their own.

Good Old Boys tend to hire other men who act as they do because they want to surround themselves with people to whom they can relate.

Hiring a Good Old Boy who would be fun to hang out with, rather than promoting a female, is just what Dexter did. There was an opening for a new district manager in Dexter's region. Whomever they hired would be my new district manager.

As soon as the job opening was made public, Hank began his campaign to secure the job. Hank was acting pathetically in his pursuit to gain the favor of Dexter. It was so sad watching him humiliate himself as he did and acting like a doting idiot did not help his cause. Since Hank wasn't aware of how stupid he looked, it was rather amusing to watch—sad but entertaining. Hank was taking the art of emulating Dexter to new heights. It wasn't long before everyone in the office became amused by his stupidity.

I was fond of calling Hank Mini-Me because he wanted so bad to be just like Dexter while perfecting the art of kissing butt. Hank was obnoxious, and his track record as a financial planner was less than stellar. To have Hank as a district manager would be a nightmare. Since there was no one else in the region interested in the job, it was looking good for old Hank. It would be like having another Dexter; only this one would be the Good Old Boy to whom I would answer directly.

While discussing the woes of having Hank for our manager, someone suggested that I throw my hat in the ring, which was not something I wanted to do. After tossing it around for a while, it became clear that Dexter would have to consider me over Hank. I had a better track record and previous management experience. We all agreed that Dexter would never hire me, and that was a relief. By putting my name in as a candidate for the opening, Dexter would most likely go outside the region to find a replacement. The thought was Dexter would not be able to justify hiring Hank over me since my credentials were much better than Hank's.

We were thinking that Dexter would undoubtedly be accountable for his choice, with performance being a high priority in the company. We thought we had the perfect plan. Our only mistake was remembering that Good Old Boys always stick to-gether, and Dexter did answer to Good Old Boys who had his back. Much to our shock, Hank became our new manager—a perfect plan on paper only.

Just to annoy Dexter, I asked him why he had hired Hank when my credentials were much better than his. Being true to his Good Old Boy image, he replied, "I think Hank has a better professional look, and that was what I was trying to achieve. There doesn't need to be any other reason."

I replied, "Well, good luck then." I left the room. There was no need to continue the conversation.

Hank was a tyrant, a bigoted, arrogant pain in the backside, just as I had predicted he would be. Hank wasted no time in making my life miserable, summoning me to his office to speak to me. I went to his office when I was ready. No one signs up for an afternoon of harassment. The next day, I went to Hank's office. He stood up and closed the door, making me feel very uncomfortable, so I opened it right back up. Hank demanded I sit as he dramatically pointed to a chair. I was not going to play his stupid game. I chose to stand, which irked him to no end. Once Hank figured out, I was not there to please him in any way, he took a deep breath as if he had practiced and puffed out his chest. Hank asked me if I knew why Dexter had hired him and not me. Before he could say another word, I replied to him, "You got the job for only one reason: you stand up when you pee, and you kiss his a@@. Is that simple enough for you?"

The poor little Good Old Boy looked like he had had the air knocked out of him. His face became bright red, his bald head broke into a sweat, and he was speechless. I had no more to say and started to head out of the door when I suddenly heard an outraged voice say, "You are wrong! Dexter chose me because he doesn't like you."

"You don't say? Is that the only reason he gave you? Well, I have a news flash for you: everyone knows Dexter does not like me, so he settled for you. Have a beautiful day."

For the next few weeks, Hank did everything he could to undermine and embarrass me and to put me down. It most often was done in front of a group of people. Hank did not attempt to be subtle. He had no reason to. Dexter had given him the green light to "take me down." Hank was vicious, always in my face, and he went for the throat, trying to be as hurtful as possible. If Hank intended to make me cry, the reason he was so cruel, it didn't work.

Hank's rude behavior became noticeable to many of the people in the office. One person who noticed was Sally, the other district manager in the office. As a woman, Sally had experienced much of the same discrimination from the Good Old Boys as I had. Sally was a brilliant and strong woman. She took matters into her own hands and arranged for me to transfer to her district. The district managers earn income from the production of the advisers—the higher the production, the higher the pay.

When Sally presented her request to have me transferred to her district, Hank did not like that. He said Sally would have to replace the income he would lose by my departure. Sally did some calculations and offered him three men from her district in exchange for me. Now Hank's only concern was not having me available for his abuse, and I suppose he was addicted to it by that point. Like a Good Old Boy, he felt entitled to handing out abuse to women.

Once the negotiations were complete, I was so happy I cried tears of joy and relief. Once I heard that Sally had to trade three men in exchange for me, I reminded him of how important I was and that it took three men to replace me every opportunity I got.

I thought the days of Hank yelling in my face were over. I should have known better. Merely three weeks later, Hank cornered me in the office and started to berate me for no reason, especially since he was no longer my manager. He was in my face, so close his nose nearly bumped into mine. He was yelling so loudly his voice carried to the other end of the office, where Dexter's office was. Dexter did not do anything to stop the commotion or even to check and see what was happening. It was almost as if he already knew what it was.

Sally could also hear the booming voice in her office and immediately stepped out to see what was happening.

When Sally saw that Hank was yelling at me and was right in my face, she walked up to him and told him to stop it. She reminded him that he was no longer my manager. Hank did not even pause. Instead, he continued to berate me, calling me foul names and using terrible language. Sally saw that Hank was not going to stop and marched right down to Dexter's office to tell him to put an end to it. Dexter did not so much as lift his head from what he was reading. He said nothing. Dexter knew what Hank was doing and saw no reason to stop him.

Hank was not letting up, so I began to walk backward toward the small cubicle area that had a chair with a surface to write and cubicle walls on both sides of the chair—not much room, but Hank could not be in my face there. Instead, Hank leaned over me, blocking me from leaving and holding me hostage in that space.

It wasn't until another male adviser walked into the area and saw what Hank was doing that, I could get free. This adviser was a very nice gentleman, not a Good Old Boy in any way. Mike had always been friendly to me and polite. He was agitated with what Hank was doing. Mike took control immediately and approached Hank. He told him to back off and leave me alone. Mike told Hank that he was out of line and would be lucky if I didn't press charges on him, and he would be happy to be a witness.

Thank goodness for gentlemen like Mike. If he had not intervened, it is hard to say what Hank might have done, knowing that he had the blessing of the regional vice president to do whatever he wanted, and there would be no consequences. Hank's behavior was ultimately out of control, yet not one person was concerned about it. Because everyone in the chain of command above him was also a Good Old Boy, and they always looked out for each other, my only solution was to carry pepper spray and make sure Hank knew I had it, so I showed my pepper spray to Hank and told him if he ever invaded my personal space, I would spray it right in his smug face.

CHAPTER 11

The Numbers Game

The numbers were the name of the game. They compiled and posted them every week with special attention for each month as well, the grand finale being the year-end results. Working as a financial planner involves sales of investments like stocks, bonds, mutual funds, and insurance. An excellent retirement planner will sell only the investments that best suit the client. There should be no thought as to which investments pay a higher commission or no commission at all. That was how I performed my job, often implementing investments that did not pay a commission at all. If that was the best solution, that was what I gave my clients.

My business practice of putting the client first should have made all the management above me pleased. However, these Good Old Boys were not pleased with my results and had no qualms about telling me. The big question was always why I had used investments that paid such low commissions. As I thought about this, this question appeared to be a direct contradiction to their desire for me to have smaller production numbers, not to mention that they were encouraging me to ignore the rule of always having the client's best interest in mind. What a dilemma. They wanted the other Good Old Boys to surpass me in production numbers, yet they were upset that I didn't use what would pay a higher commission. The Good Old Boys wanted my numbers higher to benefit their paycheck while their meeting production goals. I wished those Good Old Boys would make up their minds, and it appeared they wanted to have their cake and eat it too.

The numbers game was significant in our office. Waiting for the results was the top activity each Friday. I always thought it was foolish and a waste of time. I had been working for the company for a long time before I even knew what the numbers game was and why it was so important. I spent my time on Fridays working. What a unique idea that was.

Meanwhile, at the office, the Good Old Boys all sat around their computers, waiting for the results. Once the email with the results came in, the Good Old Boys would spend the rest of the day analyzing it. If only they would spend that much time analyzing their client's portfolios! I didn't know what they were looking for or what made it so remarkable, until one memorable day.

Out of the blue, I received a phone call from Dexter's secretary. Dexter would like me to come to his office immediately, as he wanted to talk to me. I was expected to drop everything, including scheduled appointments, and come to Dexter's office. I was sure nothing good would come of this, and I could not have been more right.

With nervous anticipation, I arrived at the office, greeting the staff with a friendly hello. No sooner were the words out of my mouth than Dexter gruffly bellowed for me to come into the office. The sound of his voice told me that I had good reason to be frightened, and I had better get right in there. Dexter had sounded harsh in the past, but nothing compared to this day. I had never seen Dexter so enraged; I could not imagine what had caused this much ire, but I was about to find out.

I walked into Dexter's office and cheerfully said hello. It seemed to piss him off that I was cheerful. That was about to change when he snapped at me, "Sit down; this will not be pleasant."

I thought to myself, *Thanks for the warning*, and wondered, *what could this be about that is so unpleasant?* Every conversation we had was uncomfortable.

With a grand gesture, he pulled out sheets of paper that had columns of numbers with names next to them. At last, here were the infamous numbers Dexter referred to often. There were four sets of printouts: one weekly, one monthly, one quarterly, and one year-to-date. Dexter flung them at me and asked, "Do you see what is wrong with this picture?" Since I had never seen them before and didn't understand what they represented, I studied the pages carefully, taking more time doing so than Dexter had patience.

Dexter exploded with anger when I told him that I did not see what was wrong. He snarled at me, "Are you so stupid that I have to tell you what is wrong?"

Since I didn't know, I responded, "I suppose you do need to tell me."

He yelled at me that these numbers represented the rankings

of everyone in the region. Well, I could see that, and yet I still did not know what the problem was. What I said next was a huge mistake. I very sweetly told him, "My name seems to appear near the top of all of the columns, and the names are not in alphabetical order."

Dexter lost his patience, his composure, and his good sense. Dexter was out of control by this point; he was screaming at me, using profanity while explaining to me that the names were in the order of performance. Well, that seemed like a good thing for me. Now, I was perplexed. Why was he so mad? I could understand his anger if I was at the bottom of each list since that would mean I was not doing my job. He should be yelling at those Good Old Boys at the bottom of the listings. I dared to point out to Dexter that I appeared at the top of all the lists, and that to me seemed it would be a good thing, so why was he so mad?

Dexter told me that this was not a good thing because it meant that I was producing more than the Good Old Boys who worked in nearby districts. Dexter pointed out to me that these three Good Old Boys were consistently lagging, and something needed to change. He said, "This is not equitable." I was not sure what he meant by that. When I asked, he said, "If this is equitable, then everyone should rank at or near the same place on the list."

I thought he was referring to the size of our book of business, which was also on the graph. I pointed out, "Each of these men has a substantially larger book of business than I have." I told him I didn't know how this situation could be inequitable. They all had many more clients than I had.

Now Dexter was perplexed, and he didn't know what had just happened. Somehow, I had turned the tables on him, and he did not like that. I repeated, "These men all have many more clients than I do, so if there is any inequality, it is against me." I probably went too far by saying that. The conversation was not going as he had planned, and he didn't know how to turn it around. You can't argue with logic—well, at least most people can't. His original plan was to take more clients from my book and add them to his Good Old Boys' books. His logic was that I was making much more money than his Good Old Boys, and it was unfair.

Dexter thought about what I had said. He asked me if I knew why I was making more money than the other men, even with a smaller book of business. I didn't have to think about that at all. I told him these men were not working as many hours as I was and didn't put as much effort into their work. Dexter knew this to be accurate but was determined to do what he wanted. What Dexter said next didn't make sense, but why should it? I knew he would do what he wanted, and this farce of a meeting was just a pretense. I could not believe what I was hearing when Dexter told me that I had better clients than the others. He thought I had better clients, and because of that, I was able to produce much more than the others. And that was where the inequity lay.

Dexter informed me that he would be reducing my book and dividing it between the other men who were at the bottom of his charts. Once they had better clients to work with, life would be more equitable.

I knew it would be a losing battle. Dexter would win. So, I got up and walked toward the door. Dexter wasn't finished with me and shouted, "Where do you think you are going? I have not dismissed you."

I didn't respond and kept walking. There was one battle he would never win, and that was, he would never see me cry.

CHAPTER 12

Ricky the Snake

Good Old Boys are the same in that they all follow the same ideals regarding women. All Good Old Boys keep the glass ceiling firmly in place. How they bully women varies with each Old Boy, each one having his own specific style and manners he exhibits. The most challenging behavior for women is passive-aggressive. This behavior can be deceptive, making it very easy to fall into their trap.

When a Good Old Boy uses passive-aggressive behavior, it is much like a sneaky snake, who will attack suddenly, giving no notice. There was one Good Old Boy in our office who had earned the name of Snake, and he fit the description perfectly. I called him Ricky the Snake, or the Snake, for short. If you referred to someone in our office as "the snake," almost everyone knew you were referring to Ricky. Dexter also knew that Ricky was a snake and took advantage of it. If Ricky had done something nasty to any of the advisers, Dexter had his back.

Complaining about Ricky to Dexter was like talking to a brick wall.

Ricky was exceptionally passive-aggressive. While he was outwardly friendly, he always had an ulterior motive when he did anything. Ricky was a Good Old Boy and was adept in the art of deception. He was a smooth talker and extremely adept at making you believe he was your friend. Once Ricky had gained your confidence, he would strike. It was not a matter of if but when. Ricky did all of this with Dexter's blessing. With a wink and a nod from Dexter, Ricky was free to pull any scam he liked. You had to be very diligent when Ricky was around. He couldn't be trusted and would lie to you with a smile on his face.

When I first started to work for the company where Dexter and Ricky worked, Ricky wasted no time trying to be my friend. He was persuasive, and I was unaware of his reputation. It didn't take him long to gain my trust. Ricky came on as a trustworthy guy who only wanted to help. No one warned me about him; he snared me in his web of lies, and I learned fast not to trust him again.

Good Old Boys like Ricky are the most devious and despicable of them all. When a male coworker comes on as charming and helpful, chances are he is up to no good. Undoubtedly, this is not true in all cases, and it is unfair to the gentlemen to lump them all in one big pot. The only problem is you don't know whom to trust.

As I said, Ricky was the most dangerous snake in the swamp. I received three school districts; all were exclusively mine to service. There was a steadfast rule that was company policy: financial advisers were supposed to market only to their school districts. There was no reason for you to go into a school district that you did not have in your book of business. This rule made sense and was a simple one to abide by unless you were a snake. Ricky did not attempt to follow this rule and took advantage of every opportunity available to get in front of the employees in one of my school districts. Ricky went as far as offering to receive calls for me while I was on vacation. His offer should have been a red flag to me, but I missed it. When I left for vacation, I had no idea what would be waiting for me when I returned. Taking full advantage of my absence, Ricky had called several of my clients and set up appointments with them, ignoring the rule of no soliciting at school districts that were not yours.

Unbeknownst to me, Ricky desired to have my largest district as his own, which was the reason he volunteered to cover for me while I was away. That should have been a red flag. However, I missed it as I had so many other red flags. Ricky went on an all-out mission to get as many of the employees in his name as possible. Now Ricky had a foothold in the school district, and there was no stopping him.

Every year in the fall, we had calendars printed. The office did the ordering, and our names and phone numbers appeared on the back of each calendar. Having your name and number at their fingertips is an excellent way to get yourself in front of potential new clients. These calendars are a bit costly, but they are useful and worth the cost.

When my order of calendars arrived, I wasted no time going to the school districts to hand them out. Imagine my surprise when I went into each school building only to find out everyone already had a calendar. How strange that seemed since the order had only come that same day. I asked to see one, with the thought that maybe they had been shipped directly to the school district. Of course, that wasn't at all what had happened. The name on each one was Ricky's, and he had given them out the week before.

It was apparent that Ricky had gotten his supply before anyone else had. I smelled a rat and went straight to Dexter's office. Indeed, he must have been behind this. I might just as well have knocked my head against the wall as to expect anything from Dexter. You would think I would have learned by now that it does no good to complain about Ricky.

When I told Dexter what Ricky had done, Dexter chastised me, saying me I was making a big deal out of nothing. In my defense, I replied to him that because of the calendar with Ricky's name and phone number, clients would expect to call him. Again, he chastised me, saying to me it didn't matter whose name was on the calendar, if the company name was on the front. Score a significant victory for Ricky.

When the Good Old Boys are in control, as they almost always are, it is a battle you can't win. Don't waste your time trying, use that time to push forward, and better yourself, despite the Good Old Boys, and leave them sputtering in your dust.

CHAPTER 13

Jessie the Con Man

Good Old Boys all have a unique talent. Jessie's ability was being a con man, and he was very good at conning people. He would charm the pants off you and pull a scam on you while he was doing it. It is difficult to protect yourself from men like Jessie. Many serial criminals are charming, and that is how they get away with much of what they do.

Jessie found it especially easy to con older people, often selling them investments that were much too risky for them, but they paid a higher commission. You don't have to be actively working to be accosted by the Good Old Boys. They will gladly come to you, where they will pour on the charm and turn your world upside down—and not in a positive way.

I found myself cleaning up after these Good Old Boys when they took advantage of the elderly. My expertise is retirement planning and wealth management. After senior citizens had been taken advantage of by a Good Old Boy, I tried to help them undo what the Old Boys had done. There were many times I helped the seniors get out of investments that were not suited for their age or risk tolerance. My belief is "Never mess with the old people."

When you retire, your information is readily available, and you probably have noticed that your mailbox is suddenly filled with invitations to free dinners. In many states, it is not an accepted practice to offer a free dinner while giving a seminar promoting your services. Very simply put, that is a form of bribery. Most, but not all, invitations come from charming Good Old Boys. Beware of free food; nothing in life is free, and there is no free lunch. The free meal is an opportunity to sell you, the attendee, investments and services.

Jessie was always planning a scheme or trying to cover up his project. He is not unlike many advisers. I am thankful there are more honest advisers than con men. On occasion, the Good Old Boys who pull a con job get busted. When caught, an insignificant fine, along with a two-year suspension of their licenses, will be the only penalties they will receive. The penalty is negligible when you compare it to how much income they derive from their scam. After a two-year vacation, they are right back at it.

Jessie had a passive-aggressive personality, which seems to be a common trait for Good Old Boys. Men like Jessie suppress women as well as con clients. You might say they are multitalented but not in the right way. The only defense, again, is being on the offense, which might seem like a full-time job. Being diligent is the only way to survive in a man's world. Never let your guard down; you never know when a Good Old Boy will strike.

Jessie was the office con man, and Clyde was the office pervert. All the offices have at least one of each, sometimes even more. It is anyone's guess which is worse, the con man or the sex offender.

Sexual perverts are irrepressible, and they have no boundaries. Most perverted men are rash, and once they get you alone, they become dangerous. Because of this behavior, it is necessary to have zero tolerance for any of their advances, no matter how innocent they appear. Well, there is never any reason for a male to touch you! Anything that makes you feel uncomfortable is strictly forbidden. When a pervert tries to touch you, you need to tell the offender that he is never to touch any part of your body again. If the pervert makes another attempt to touch you, report him immediately. The three-times-and-you're-out-rule does not apply in this situation.

Most sinister offenders like to challenge you and have no self-control. These perverts will not stop this bad behavior on their own. Turning them in is your only option. You can't possibly deal with these individuals yourself. While sitting at my desk, a Good Old Boy came from behind to rub my shoulders. When told to stop, he became outraged and agitated. These Good Old Boys do not like to hear the word *no*, especially from a woman. When a Good Old Boy hears no, he will immediately turn the tables on you, saying you are blowing things out of proportion. Don't fall for that. Remember, no man has a right to touch a woman, period. Anything that makes you uncomfortable is forbidden. It is not possible to believe that it is blowing anything out of proportion.

These Good Old Boys have become experts on covering their butts and almost always have another Good Old Boy to cover for them. These Good Old Boys are predators and look for women who appear weak. Never give anyone the impression that you are vulnerable. If a predator gets the impression that you are, he will swoop down on you like flies on a cow pie.

Strong women are seldom the target for sexual predators; most predators are intimidated by strong women and will avoid them. Keeping a predator away from you is the best defense possible. Just think of being self-confident as taking control away from someone who intends to harm you.

You need to stay in control of every situation. It is the only way to be diligent regarding your safety. As parents, we teach our teenagers these rules for safety and yet fail to follow them ourselves.

One of the offices that I worked in had a deviant predator. This Good Old Boy approached me while I was walking down the hallway. Before I knew what was happening, he reached out and touched me on the chest. I was shocked and frightened by his boldness, and he had taken me by surprise. Before I was able to speak, a loud and angry voice bellowed out from behind me. "Don't touch that woman! I will see you in my office!"

The sudden anger and authority in Tim's voice were enough to stop my would-be attacker dead in his tracks. I felt I had dodged a bullet that day. Had Tim not been right behind me, heaven only knows what might have happened. I was preoccupied while walking down the hallway and let my guard down. I felt safe because I was in the office where I worked.

I should have known better and believing that a man is sweet, and innocent based on appearances is a big mistake. Remember that men, especially Good Old Boys, think with their little head.

CHAPTER 14

The Arrogant Man

We all know at least one arrogant man. Usually, we know several. We understand what it means, as well. But do we know the ways to describe it? Here are six descriptive words that all translate to arrogance.

1. Conceited feeling self-important
2. Ostentatious—fond of making a pretentious display of vanity
3. Haughty—disdainful and overbearingly proud
4. Insolent—arrogant and disrespectful toward others, especially women
5. Dictatorial speaking in an overbearing manner, bullying
6. Bumptious—pushy, proud, noisily self-assertive, brazen, cheeky, impertinent, and nervy, (this is a favorite one)

All these words describe arrogance. Most individuals exhibit just one or two of these attributes. Very rarely will you find an individual who exhibits all of them. I was unfortunate enough to meet the rare person who did. His name was Sam, and he was an attorney. I have met some very pretentious Good Old Boys in my lifetime, but not one of them could hold a candle to Sam. Sadly enough, Sam didn't even know he was arrogant, strutting through life as though he were royalty, expecting that everyone who met him would automatically realize he was the best, most consequential person in the universe.

Sam often spoke in the third person, envisioning that this was routine for a person as unique as he thought he was.

When I required the help of a lawyer for a medical malpractice suit, I hired Sam, based on a recommendation of someone I thought to be reliable. I know now it was a terrible mistake. The fact that I hired Sam, which would mean that he worked for me, escaped Sam entirely.

Sam acted as if it was a privilege that I was able to hire him and have him argue my case. Sam had his staff send me the paperwork that was necessary to begin the litigation. I was expecting to meet him and discuss my lawsuit, but Sam was much too busy with important business to spare the time necessary to bother with me.

Every time I tried to call him, I got his voice mail, and on the rare occasion that he answered the call, he was condescending and always managed to put me off. He made it clear that he was in control and would tell me what was happening in my case on a need-to-know basis.

When Sam answered my emails, which he did not always do, he would start them out with, "These types of emails are not productive." Asking him questions regarding the procedures of my ongoing case was not unproductive: it was his job to answer my questions. Sam did not want to hear that or anything I had to say. When he did reply to an email, he would often include sentences like, "Note to self, doesn't everybody already know this?" Communicating with him became impossible. I felt he represented the other side most of the time. Sam would go weeks without talking to me, causing me to wonder what was going on.

Soon the weeks turned to months that turned to years. As time went on, Sam became more obnoxious and started to be outright rude with his put-downs.

Suddenly one day, I received a notice of the date and time of my deposition. I was not sure what this would involve. I had never been a party to a lawsuit. I had no idea what to expect, and that made me extremely nervous. I made several attempts to contact Sam. None were successful.

Not knowing what to expect, I arrived at the law firm, found the conference room indicated in my letter, went in, and took a seat. After I spent several minutes listening to myself breathe, a woman walked into the room, introduced herself, and told me she was there to represent me for the deposition. I had never seen this woman before, and I assumed that she had made a mistake or that I was in the wrong room. I informed her that my lawyer was Sam, and he would be representing me. She smiled and told me that she would fill in for Sam for the deposition. She explained that Sam could not be there. Sam was away attending to important business—as if this were just for shits and giggles. This deposition was significant. Why was he blowing me off again? As it turned out, Linda was not only filling in for Sam—she was taking over the case. Sam had passed me to Linda without so much as a warning. All future correspondence now came from Linda's office.

It was my understanding that I had signed a contract with Sam, allowing Sam to represent me. Nowhere on the contract did it say that Sam could turn my case over to another lawyer. When I received any legal documents, Sam's name appeared as my attorney.

Sam is a Good Old Boy like no other Good Old Boy. He has no respect for women, and he thinks he is a god. I endured two years and nine months of inept representation. I hired one lawyer whose expertise was supposed to be in medical malpractice, only to end up with an attorney who had never argued a medical malpractice suit.

After more than two years since signing the contract, I received a letter that announced my lawsuit was going to mediation and listed the date, time, and location—another shocking surprise. No one had discussed this with me, and I had no idea this was going to happen.

I was looking carefully at the letter, and I discovered Sam's name listed as my attorney. Seeing this, I wasted no time in calling Sam. I asked Sam what I should expect from the upcoming mediation that I knew nothing about and told him that I also had some other questions. His quick response was for me to call Linda and set up an appointment to meet with her to discuss it. He was going to pass me over to Linda again, dismissing me as if I were mud on his shoes.

I was getting tired of this and asked him if he too would be at this meeting with Linda since his name appeared on the letter as my attorney and Linda's did not. Sam did not expect this question and had no time to prepare an excuse. He quickly answered, "Of course, I will be there; why would you even have to ask?" I told him I had to ask because this case was over two and a half years in the making, and I had still had not met him. He had dismissed me and passed me on to others. I wasn't sure if he would do the same with this meeting.

On the day of the mediation, I walked into an enormous conference room, big enough to seat a dozen people or more. Linda was already there and waiting for me. Sam was not present, and I was not surprised. I was sure he would stand me up, and it appeared I was right. Without wasting time, Linda quickly got down to business. We had been talking for more than ten minutes before Sam made his grand entrance. You would think that royalty had just entered the room. I swear I heard the trumpeters announce his coming. Not knowing if I should bow or curtsy, I remained in my chair. Before Sam could speak, I asked him straight out if he would have been there if I had not asked him if he was coming. Sam did not expect that I would ask him this and was speechless, for the first time in his life, I would guess.

Regaining his composure, Sam said, "Of course I planned to come. Why would you ask? Didn't I tell you I was coming?"

"Yes, you did," I replied, "but I really can't believe you when you speak to me. Your past behavior speaks for itself."

Sam was very annoyed at my response and made no further comment.

For the duration of the meeting, he didn't say a word, leaving everything up to Linda. His demeanor was impassive, and he continuously checked his watch. By his body language, Sam was sending a clear message that he had better things to do with his time. It was like being in a room with a spoiled child.

Sam thinks that he is an aristocrat, particularly when it comes to women. He has the patience of a gnat and the disposition of a bulldog. In Sam's mind, the glass ceiling is bulletproof, and it will not incur even a tiny crack if he is around. I have no doubt there are hundreds of men who act like Sam. It just so happens that I experienced his deplorable disposition firsthand.

There are many different degrees of Good Old Boys, from mild to exceedingly awful. I hope you never meet a Good Old Boy like Sam. If you should not be so lucky, hold your position, don't show fear, and remember that you do have a voice.

Even when men and women work at the same job, they each have a different set of rules to follow. These rules can change at the drop of a hat, and many of them are unwritten rules, making them seem very ambiguous, but they always favor the Good Old Boys. While men receive promotions, women are only bumping their heads on the glass ceiling. Nothing has changed, nor will it anytime soon.

Why do men act chauvinistically? That is the question of the day. Several possibilities may all be the actual answer. The reasons are different with each man. They form a brotherhood that is strong and anchored on unquestioned trust and secrecy. Most Good Old Boys have a dislike toward strong, intelligent women who are confident and secure.

The higher the level of education, the cleverer the Old Boy is. Having a degree and qualifications for a high-paying job does not protect you from a Good Old Boy. You are more likely to run into a Good Old Boy at a high-end job. Sometimes, Good Old Boys work behind the scenes; you cannot see them or watch what they are doing but have no doubts; they are there.

An excellent example is the story of my friend Marie, who is the chairperson of the world languages department at a top-rated college where she teaches. Marie has a doctorate, as do many of the males who chair a department.

A list of names of the department chairpersons compiled for a brochure gave credit to those who held a doctorate. Under closer observation, Marie noticed that everyone given credit were men. Marie was not given credit for having a doctorate. She was also the only woman who was a chairperson. Could this have been an oversight? Or was this the work of a Good Old Boy behind the scenes. We will never know for sure.

When Marie pointed out to the staff that she had not been given credit for also holding a doctorate, she was dismissed and told that it would be too costly to reprint the brochures for just the one mistake. Had that been a male they had overlooked; would they have been so dismissive? Most likely not.

This example is one way of keeping women from joining the ranks of the Good Old Boys. Continuing to keep women in their place is how the Good Old Boys see it.

Another great example is that of a female doctor who shared an office with three male doctors. It should not be a surprise at this point to know that it was her job to make the coffee before the male doctors arrived at the office and to keep the coffee machine clean and stocked with coffee. Will these Good Old Boys ever get over the coffee stigma? Most undoubtedly not.

Male dominance is also present in families. An example of that is caring for aging parents. It appears to be an unwritten rule that the females of the family are designated caregivers. Even if the female sibling lives a distance away, while her brothers live close by, the responsibility of caring for the parents will lie on the sister.

The male siblings will often give the excuse that they must work and are busy, knowing full well that their sister also works, is active, and will have to spend hours in the car for a round-trip visit. I am not sure if they are ignorant of the full impact it has on their sister or if they don't care and consider it her duty. The answer lies somewhere in the middle.

When it comes to inheritance, the boys are the first ones in line with their hands out, waiting to get their share. Although sad, it happens across the country regularly. It seems to be a generational tradition, and that will not change either.

Many of the Good Old Boys will boast of their chauvinistic ways and pride themselves on how badass they are, until one day another Good Old Boy treats their wife or daughter the way they treat women.

With the knowledge of their wife or daughter bullied by a Good Old Boy, a change in the attitude of that Good Old Boy might occur, but don't hold your breath. It is hard to teach an old dog new tricks. Most of the Good Old Boys live in denial. They think they have done no wrong. They act like cowards, sticking their heads in the sand. The result of this is their behinds are exposed. They are a bunch of dumb asses.

CHAPTER 15

The Phone Call that Changed My Life

When Good Old Boys feel intimidated by a woman, they freak out and act impulsively. Their egos are like fine china and will crack with the slightest amount of pressure. Good Old Boys are used to getting their way, especially from women, since they believe they are far superior to any woman. When a Good Old Boy decides he doesn't want a woman around to intimidate him, the Good Old Boy will do almost anything to rid himself of her presence.

The double standard rule plays a big part in his endeavor to remove her from his work environment. He is using every trick at his disposal, such as privilege and cooperation from his band of brothers, the Good Old Boys. The Good Old Boys will help each other at any cost, sometimes even breaking the law or merely doing something unethical.

The Good Old Boys have no fear and hold nothing back when they have a mission to accomplish. They need not be concerned about punishment or consequence because most likely, their immediate supervisor is also a Good Old Boy, who will help him with his mission.

When I resigned from the Fortune 500 company where I had worked for twenty years, I became an independent financial adviser. I would no longer have a manager to make my life miserable. Instead, I would only need to comply with the rules of investment through a broker-dealer. There would be a compliance officer, known as a principal, from the broker-dealer, approving all my trades and investments for accuracy and making sure they were appropriate for the client. I would see this person only once a year. Working as an independent was just what I was looking for, and I was confident that it would work for me.

Working as an independent had its downfalls; I no longer had a professional office where I could meet with my clients. But I worked that out as soon as I got started. I usually met with clients at their office or home, and a friend from way back offered me her conference room to use if I came across a client who insisted on meeting at my office.

Working as a financial adviser requires that I renew my licenses every year. I had several and was glad to know that the broker-dealer kept track of this and would just send me a notice when they were about to expire. I had the fees deducted from my paycheck and was good for another year. The fact that the broker-dealer did that for me was a great relief. The rules are stringent for securities licensing; there is a deadline for payment, which must clear before midnight of the due date, and there are no exceptions. There are no second chances. If money is not received, the cancellation of your license is the penalty. Having your license canceled would mean having to take the exams all over again, and new ones would be issued when you pass each exam. There was no way I was ever going to be late on my payments. The threat of losing my licenses was genuine, and I got it. The importance of meeting their deadline is the difference between working and not working.

Every year, I paid my renewal fees and received an email confirming that the payment was received. The process the broker-dealer used was working like clockwork since I had become independent. That is, until one memorable year when I paid my fees as soon as I received notice, which was well in advance of the deadline. I received the paid-in-full receipt, as I always had in the past. Nothing seemed to be out of the ordinary; I continued to conduct business as usual.

Then one day, I received a notification directly from the service company that filed the renewals. It said that my renewal fees were still due. That seemed odd to me since I had received my notice of receipt from the broker-dealer more than two weeks before I received the notice. Fearing the loss of my licenses, I called the broker-dealer to inquire why I had gotten the notification saying I had not paid. I also forwarded a copy of my paid-in-full receipt. The young gentleman who answered the phone put me on hold so that he could check into it. After several minutes, he returned and told me rather curtly that I had paid and proof of that was the receipt that he had sent me. He followed it up by sending me a memo showing that my balance was zero.

I had a very uncomfortable feeling about this, and as if to

confirm my worries, two days later, I received another notice, also telling me that I had not paid my fees, and the deadline was now fast approaching.

This second notice put the fear of God in me, and I reluctantly called the broker-deal again. The same young man answered the phone and immediately became irritated when I told him my name and why I was calling. I told him I was calling because this was a second notice, and the deadline was coming up very quickly.

The Good Old Boy said a check and a list of names of the advisers who paid went to the agency. I asked him if he was sure my name was on that list. Hearing me say this was more than the Good Old Boy could handle. He snapped at me that my name was obviously on the list because I had paid, and I had a receipt from him telling me that I had a zero balance, so what more could he do for me?

I did not like the way he was handling this, but it would be of no use to complain to anyone about him; he was a Good Old Boy, and his superiors were also Good Old Boys.

When I received another notice the following day that I had still not paid my fees, I called the young man at the broker-dealer once again, only to hear the same excuse as the day before.

By this time, I was in a panic. It seemed to me that someone was trying to force me to lose my license. I decided to take matters into my own hands. I called the agency that was sending me the notices to ask them why I was receiving these notices when I had paid my fees to the broker-dealer. They told me that they had sent them a check with a list of all the advisers who had already paid.

The clerk at the agency was accommodating. She put me on

hold so she could check into it and give me an answer. It wasn't long before the clerk was back on the phone. She told me that my name was not on the list and offered to fax me a copy of the list. When I received a copy of the record, I checked for my name, and sure enough, it was not there.

Seeing the copy, I was sent and not finding my name on it gave me a very sick feeling. Now I was sure someone was trying to sabotage me.

Now it was my turn to be irate. That Good Old Boy answering the phone had not checked to see if my name was on the list as he had said he did. He lied. Before I called the Good Old Boy back, I faxed him the report I had received from the agency. When I made my call, I wanted him to have my copy in his hands, thinking this would prevent further lying. The deadline was now just seventy-two hours away. I was running out of time, and this now required desperate measures.

When I called the broker-dealer back, a different Good Old Boy answered. This Good Old Boy was the supervisor of the department. His name was Theodore, and he had an attitude that was so defensive I thought I might have called the military by mistake. Of course, I had not made a mistake, and Mr. Theodore was about to chastise me by starting his conversation with "There is no need for you to be so angry. There was a human error, but we found it in time."

I replied, "Only because I got to the bottom of it by calling the agency. Who do you think sent you that report? Look closely; it came from me."

Theodore became hostile, telling me that my name was not the only name that they had missed: there were three others, all men.

I let him know I didn't care if there were three or three thousand; I was concerned about only my name. Telling me I was not the only one who did not make it on the list did not make me feel better.

Theodore told me that no harm had occurred; the fees would be remitted for me as well as the other three and with time to spare. Theodore also told me that he did not appreciate my attitude. It was a human mistake, and it was corrected, so there was no reason to get my feathers ruffled.

Okay, now he had gone too far. To put it simply, I lost it, big time. I was furious. I did not curse or swear at him. I did control myself enough to get my point across without becoming vulgar. I told him I did not appreciate his thoughtless attitude. I said, "I was lied to and dismissed, and all the while, I was in danger of losing my license. If I had not called the agency, you would never have admitted your mistake. The deadline would come and go, and I would be out of a job. That is unacceptable behavior." I also might have called him stupid or maybe a dumb ass.

Theodore was not going to accept that he had done anything wrong. Hearing that, I called him a stooge and told him a monkey could do his job better. I believe anyone in my position would have been equally as annoyed and told him what was on their mind. As it turned out, the three other men did just that. These three men who also were missing from the list were even angrier than I was. These men were extremely out of control when they called Theodore. They appeared to be very hostile. They, too, had almost lost their licenses.

With my licenses safely intact, I went about my business, feeling very grateful that it had ended well. It seemed that my life was back to normal, and I had some inspiring plans for my future. Life was good.

My life was about to turn upside down with one phone call. I could never have imagined that just one week later, all hell would break loose. Then it happened. The phone rang, and I answered with a cheerful hello, the only word I said. I was not allowed to say anything else. This call was short but not too sweet. The caller was demanding I submit my resignation letter by the next day. The Good Old Boy on the phone gave no reason, nor was I told who was requesting it. The only thing he said was that I needed to turn in my letter of resignation by the next day. If I chose not to, they would do it for me, and he hung up.

I was in shock and could not believe this could happen. My work ethics were stellar. I had never received a client complaint or had a compliance issue. My production was tops in the company. I had done nothing wrong, nothing at all. None of that mattered. I was a woman, and I had spoken disrespectfully to Theodore, and he was a supervisor. It was not acceptable for a woman to disrespect a man in authority. A man could disrespect him, but not a woman.

The other three men had been abusive and vulgar, not to mention they had also threatened to kick his ass. These men were not in trouble because men have anger issues that women don't, so they were just acting like men.

What had just happened to me impacted me so severely that I lost confidence and became very depressed. I had less than one week to sign on to another broker-dealer, before the Christmas break. The office staff of the agency that transfers licenses from one broker-dealer to another would be off on break for three weeks. I did not have three weeks. I had to be registered with a new broker-dealer before the vacation started.

The task of transferring to another broker-dealer seemed insurmountable. There were so many things to do and so little time to do them. I would have a mountain of papers to fill out, and a new set of fingerprints were in order, as was another background check. Although not a problem, it would be time-consuming.

Getting everything done created a tremendous amount of stress, especially since I was severely depressed and had little confidence in myself. It could not have happened at a worse time. The day I got the call was my son's birthday, and it was just before Christmas.

Until that call, I had lots of energy and was very positive. Then it was gone. I could barely put one foot in front of the other. Knowing that quitting was not an option, I tried my best to move forward. I put everything in God's hands and trusted that He would guide me through this, and all would be okay soon. My grandmother used to say, "This too shall pass."

The double standard was so transparent: when the men called, screamed, and used profanity, it was acceptable because men are unable to control their anger. I started to think about retiring, but that would mean I had let the Good Old Boys win, and that just was not going to happen on my watch.

I would find the strength and move forward with God's help. After I had gotten over the initial shock, I was able to plan for my next move strategically. I was determined to continue working as an independent. I had no desire to work side by side with the Good Old Boys ever again. Working as an independent would not be perfect by any means, but it would eliminate working directly with incorrigible Good Old Boys.

Enduring the constant formidable behavior of the multitude of Good Old Boys I had encountered was starting to take a toll on my health. If I continued to work as a financial planner, I would have to work smarter. I would not immerse myself in work as I had done before. I would start by transferring my squeaky wheels to another financial planner, one who was much younger than I was. I tried to eliminate as much of the stress from my life as possible. My days of competing with the Good Old Boys had to come to an end.

There would be no more top producer events and trips for me to attend. That would eliminate the opportunities for the boys to put me down as they did the year, I was in the top ten in the country. Every year, there was a convention held to honor the top 225 producers and their significant others. The location was always a five-star hotel at a lush and usually tropical location. Admittedly, I always looked forward to the adventure. I was able to go to places that I would never have gone on my own. It was a week of exciting activities and good food, along with a never-ending supply of adult beverages.

The climax of the convention is a dinner and awards banquet. Money was not an issue for these events. They did an excellent job of putting on the Ritz.

After dinner, the awards ceremony began with recognition of the fifty highest-ranking advisers. Following that, the identification of the top ten advisers took place, along with a short story of their accomplishments. A photographer snapped some pictures of each of the ten advisers. I was one of those ten that year. Once the photographer had finished snapping photos of the ten advisers, he called the remaining forty advisers to join us on the stage for a group photo. The photographer gave explicit instructions that the ten members of the presidents' cabinet stand in the center front row. As one of the ten, I made my way to the center of the front row. That was when it became a free for all. Each of these Good Old Boys had an ego big enough to fill the entire stage. There certainly was not enough room for forty-nine big egos. They were all pushing and shoving to vie for the front row, all the while elbowing me and pushing me further and further back on the stage. I ended up in the back on the far right. I am five feet five inches tall, and most of these Old Boys were over six feet tall and had the shoulders of a linebacker. I was swallowed up and became invisible to the camera.

Noticing that he could not see me, the photographer began to implore to them: "Please make room for the woman in the front row." His pleas went unheard as the boys continued to jockey for position. When the photographer realized the boys were not going to let me into the front row, he started to snap some photos. During the entire photo session, I stood up on my toes, trying to get my head between the shoulders of two giant Good Old Boys. The first time I saw the photo, I had to search carefully to find myself. I finally found myself—well, at least part of my head, poking out between the two Good Old Boys. That picture would make a great poster to show how Good Old Boys treat women.

The trips and banquets always ended up the same way. I would be excited to go, and when I got there, the Good Old Boys were exceptionally nasty, mostly because they didn't like the fact that I was even there. I was delighted to know I would never have to go to another event for the rest of my life. Evading that situation was necessary to avoid stress. A woman needs to know how to pick her battles. That is the only way to survive in a man's world.

The Good Old Boys' Club continues to grow, and sexual exploitation is as strong as ever. Most of the bad behavior remains unreported, leaving women without a voice. Men stay in power and take advantage of women, knowing there will be no consequences.

We are most certainly living in a man's world. There is an unspoken yet very real inequity among men and women. Years ago, the workplace was homogeneous with a woman's place in the home. Most of the workforce consisted of white males, and their attitude determined the culture of the office. The Good Old Boys decided who succeeded and who failed, all because they wanted to keep their membership secure. They evolved into a club of social networking and cronyism. It was imperative to keep their workplace filled with men just like themselves. In their opinion, it was the only way the world could survive. The Good Old Boys' Club is where the real work gets done and where critical decisions come about.

We need to make gender equality the new normal, and that won't be easy. The original Good Old Boys' Club is less visible, but rest assured, it is still there. I have experienced verbal and emotional abuse, as well as humiliation; I was lied to, mistreated, and had a gun pointed to my head. With all of that, I am still here to talk about it.

I hope that women will speak up and refuse to tolerate any abuse. I believe violence from men persists everywhere, knows no boundaries, and crosses over every economic threshold. Gender discrimination should become a thing of the past.

Being bullied is too high a price to pay for any job. Never

dismiss it, thinking that it will get better because it won't. It will only get worse. The faster you remove yourself from the abusive behavior, the better your life will be. If you are experiencing abuse, especially on the job, it will affect your life in ways you can't even imagine.

The first unmistakable sign is a lack of confidence. Where you once were a very confident person, you are now very insecure. When this happens, it gives your abuser more power to control you. Anxiousness will take over your life, and that is another sign. The job you once loved is no longer enjoyable. You now dread even going to work. From this point, everything will begin to spiral out of control, and the only way to stop it is to remove yourself from the situation.

There are steps that you can take to prevent an abuser from controlling you. The first step is never to let him see you cry and always seem to agree with him. Never tell him that he has upset you. To him, bullying you is nothing more than a game and another way to stroke his ego. Always be brave and show that you are confident. Put on a happy face and head straight to the bathroom. You will have privacy there and be able to cry or swear a blue streak and let off steam once you have composed yourself. Wipe away your tears and go back to work as if nothing had happened. By removing yourself, it will take the fun out harassing you, and the Good Old Boy will get no satisfaction from his actions, which could cause him to stop.

If the abuse has begun to be more than control issues and has turned into devious behavior, you must go to human resources and report the offense. When you file the complaint, stick to the facts, tell the truth, and keep it short and straightforward. If you have a witness, bring that witness with you. If the human resources person is a male, it will be difficult to tell him what has happened.

There are laws on the books that make retaliation a crime. Unfortunately, those laws get ignored. It might be in your best interest to quit. Fighting a Good Old Boy who is being protected by another Good Old Boy is not a battle you are likely to win.

There is one thing I taught my children at a young age. Life is not fair. Regardless of that, you must always do the right thing. By doing the right thing, you build a reputation of being someone others can trust.

Now that you know who the Good Old Boys are and how they operate, tread carefully, and always have your guard up. Never, ever let them see you cry. You will bump your head on the glass ceiling a time or two, but never quit. Always do your best.

ABOUT THE AUTHOR

Anne Covey enjoys repurposing flea market finds, making jewelry, creating art, and spending time with her two children and granddaughter. She lives with her husband of forty-five years in Michigan.

www.ingramcontent.com/pod-product-compliance
Lightning Source LLC
Chambersburg PA
CBHW050356290526
45786CB00003B/1014